What is a Person
in the age of AI

also by
DR. JASON LEE MCKINNEY

Deconstructing a Disciple's Doubt
Devotions for Deconstructors

WHAT IS A PERSON
IN THE AGE OF AI

Dr. Jason Lee McKinney

WordCrafts Press

Publication Date: August 1, 2025

Hardback ISBN: 978-1-967649-12-9

Paperback ISBN: 978-1-967649-13-6

Cover concept by Mike Parker. Cover design by David Thomas. Watercolor art by Dann Zehr.

Published by WordCrafts Press
Cody, Wyoming 82414
www.wordcrafts.net

Contents

The rise of artificial intelligence is a game changer for how we relate to technology. AI raises practical and ethical questions about our future—questions that are currently generating a great deal of anxiety and hope. But AI also raises deeper metaphysical questions about selfhood and humanity. What does it mean to be a person? What gives human life value? Are human beings truly unique? If so, how? Though these questions are increasingly unavoidable, most people are underprepared to answer them.

Jason McKinney has written a wonderful book that walks us through the fundamental contours of human uniqueness. Emphasizing the unparalleled nature of the human person, he offers a balanced and careful analysis of AI, demonstrating that it is possible to utilize it as a tool while resisting its very real dangers.

The question driving McKinney's book is: what are the necessary conditions of selfhood? He explores various features of our humanity, including consciousness, free will, sentience, the soul, the body, and imagination. The ultimate basis for human exceptionalism, according to McKinney, is creation in the image of God. Human uniqueness is ultimately a theological reality, bestowed from above. This conviction arises not from prejudice, but from an awareness of our qualitative uniqueness, manifest in many diverse aspects of human culture and life but ultimately rooted in our relationship with our Creator.

McKinney avoids classifying AI as purely bad. It can function as a helpful tool, but it must be held in check: any wise use of AI must begin with a proper appraisal of its nature. That is what McKinney offers in this book. Along the way, the discussion raises all kinds of fascinating issues, such as the nature of angels.

The nature of AI is a topic that can no longer be avoided. Whether you are just entering the conversation or coming with a particular question in mind, I highly recommend *What is a Person in the age of AI* This is a topic that must be addressed head on. The implications are far-reaching and increasingly relevant. As we consider the reality of personhood, we come face-to-face with the most fundamental questions of life: who we are, and where we find meaning. It is only when we have clarity about our own nature that we can appreciate the wondrous and happy discovery that reality itself is Personal.

~Gavin Ortlund, PhD, Fuller Seminary

Dr. Ortlund serves as President of Truth Unites, Theologian-in-Residence at Immanuel Nashville, and Visiting Professor of Historical Theology at Phoenix Seminary. He is the author of numerous books, including *Why God Makes Sense in a World that Doesn't*.

INTRODUCTION

I recently taught an undergraduate class about copyright in a Survey of Music Business course. Copyright can get quite complex in many ways, but what constitutes an author has traditionally been straightforward. That is until recently. In 2023, a song went viral that mimicked the voices and style of artists Drake and The Weeknd. While a ghostwriter technically wrote the song, there was significant controversy because the writer wasn't just influenced by Drake and The Weeknd but used AI to data scrape their styles and voices. The song was allowed to be submitted for Grammy consideration. This was allowed because a human technically wrote the song. The Recording Academy has stated that only human creations are eligible. Further the U.S. Copyright office in 2025 further clarified in Part 2 of the Copyright and Artificial Intelligence Report that human contribution is necessary, essential, and must be perceptible for a work to meet the threshold of copyrightability. The legal issues on AI and copyright are by no means settled, however there at least seems be a stake in the ground. However, with AI song generators like Suno and LimeWire Audio the barrier to entry in order to create a professional, marketable, and historically monetizable work, has literally zeroed out. An article in *Digital News* states of Limewire, "The company says its AI Music Studio will introduce a revolutionary, easy-to-use interface that empowers individuals, regardless of their experience, to become music artists." In essence, with simple prompts, anyone can create songs with the help of AI—however, the AI will data scrape artists' past songs, including their musical and lyrical style. The entrance of AI-generated content, and where the AI get their "ideas" from, complicates the issue of who is an author both legally and ethically. When the thread of this is pulled to its conclusion, it takes the issue back to what it means to be a human.

The following is an outline of the conversation regarding copyright that took place in the classroom.

Professor: For a song created with the prompt, write me a track like Led Zeppelin but with the lyrical styling of Michael Jackson and a vocal melody like Bruno Mars. Who should be the author?

Student A: The author is the person who put in the prompts. They had the initial idea and that idea is perceptible.

Professor: Remember, ideas cannot be copyrighted. The idea must be put into a fixed form to be copyrightable, ideas are not in themselves perceptible.

Student A: Didn't they put it into a fixed form by writing the prompt?

Professor: Technically, the AI put the idea into a fixed form. Again ideas, in this case prompts, cannot be copyrighted. I could have the idea for a song about a washing machine run by aliens in the style of a gospel hymn played on the didgeridoo and phrased like Tom Waits in the key of H# at 1654bpms in 4/4 time, but I did not write a song. If you

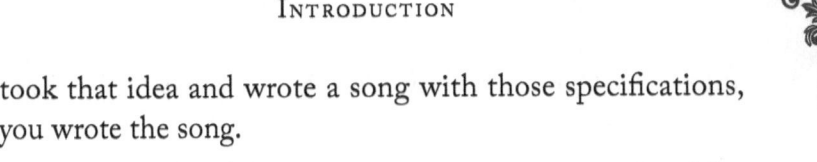

took that idea and wrote a song with those specifications, you wrote the song.

Student B: Yes, because if you (professor) didn't come up with any melody or lyrics, you didn't write the song. The lyrics and melody are what make an author.

Student A: That is true; then it would be the artists being mimicked or data scraped.

Student C: That can't be. We all mimic artists by whom we are influenced. The Beatles datascraped Carl Perkins, and countless artists have mimicked the Beatles. The AI is just better at mimicking than we are.

Student D: Then the author is the person who created the AI to begin with, right?

Professor: If you follow that logic, should I not get all my son's copyrights because he is a songwriter and recording artist? I mean, I created him.

Student A: But you didn't actively participate in writing any of your son's songs. He came up with those ideas and put them into fixed form. The songs came from his thoughts.

Student B: Even if you gave him the idea for the song, if your son wrote it, he should get the copyrights. Ideas aren't songs.

Student C: So, then the AI itself is the author? How does that work? How would AI get paid?

Professor: Only people (or groups of people incorporated) can own intellectual property... song copyrights being intellectual property, how can AI be given ownership? The copyright office has said AI created works cannot be copyrighted, but should they be? Is this the ethical stance?

Student E: For now it is, but what if AI can create content on its own without a prompt and they have or will reach the point where they are self-aware and conscious, they become a person!

Professor: The terms *human* and *person* are synonymous. To date, only humans have been granted a person or selfhood status. Are you saying AI can be human or that personhood is not necessarily tied to being a human?

Student E: I think the second one. Why is it that only humans can be persons? In the age we live in now, what gives us the right to say that only we can be persons?

The question at the heart of that final statement is, what are the necessary conditions of selfhood, and why can't AI meet them? This question is born out of the bigger, perhaps biggest, philosophical question facing contemporary culture: what does it mean to be human? Humans face this question as a kind (intrinsic to the species) and a type (specific to groups of individuals or individuals). I will go through a thought experiment where I will deconstruct philosophical assumptions about what makes a person a person. I will break down different variables often asserted as making humans different and try to determine if they are necessary. This argument might seem circular to some as I deconstruct the assumptions that humans are people. It seems like all philosophy, theology, and science have agreed, reasonably universally, that humans (at least under typical conditions) meet the criteria for selfhood. Humans possess or obtain being persons. I admit that I am starting with that assumption. I am not arguing primarily whether humans obtain selfhood if there is such a thing as selfhood. I am trying to

philosophically break down the necessary conditions that humans possess that make up selfhood and whether any other entity in existence can meet the necessary conditions to possess selfhood, particularly Artificial Intelligence.

What are the necessary conditions that make a person a person? Is it consciousness? Is it intelligence? Is it free will? Is it sentience? Or is it something physical? Is it something metaphysical? Who am I? What does it mean to be me, a human, a self, a person? What are the conditions for reaching the state of being a distinct person? There is a question behind the question of "who am I?" The more foundational question is what it means to be an "I"? What does it mean to be a self? Can AI possess the necessary conditions of selfhood? Can AI be a person?

Historically, the terms human and person have been held as synonymous. The *American Heritage Dictionary* defines the word human as a person. The contemporary scientific age has emphasized the biology of being human. Thus, a person is a biological human. But does that capture all the fundamental essence of what it means to be a person? Does biology give a whole explanation?

Contemporary thought holds that biology has nothing to do with what it means to be a person and that consciousness, or the intelligence of the soul is what truly makes a person. But do any of these completely explain what a person is by themselves?

One thing that must be clarified is that Artificial Intelligence is not just one thing; AI is not one thing. There are many kinds of AI, but the three main ones are narrow AI, general AI, and super AI. Narrow AI has a particular and limited area of knowledge. Narrow AI has been around for many years, and we all use narrow AI daily (think Spotify algorithms). General AI (or AGI) can learn tasks unprompted by humans and in a context outside of its primary programming (think learning a new language to solve shipping issues between countries better). Finally, there is super AI, which is AI that can reason abstractly and reach knowledge that far exceeds human knowledge. Many assert that super AI is/

will be self-aware of its existence as well as the world around the AI. They assert super AI will have desires and a will of its own.

I am going to break down assumptions of what selfhood is in this thought experiment. I will deconstruct assumptions and focus on reconstructing only the necessary conditions to possess or obtain selfhood. I will attempt to show what, at its core, makes a person a person. I will also show why AI cannot possess these necessary conditions. The reasons why AI should not be considered a person/granted selfhood morally both from a philosophical and theological standpoint. I am not going to argue the legal merits of AI selfhood. I am also not going to argue whether the overall impact of AI on human society and the earth is or will be more positive or negative.

The Primary Question: What are the necessary conditions of selfhood, and can AI possess them?

Vocabulary

I decided to let a chatbot create the vocabulary glossary for the book. I did this for three reasons. 1. To show that I am not anti-AI, 2. To show that AI is a great tool, and 3. To see where AI and I may disagree. All in all, AI did a pretty good job. One exception is the definition of a person. The AI said a person is "typically" human. I'm afraid I have to disagree. A second place where AI got it wrong is in the description of selfhood. The AI uses consciousness as a part of the definition of selfhood. I disagree. Interestingly, the two most important words and concepts for this book and my philosophical point are those that AI got wrong.

1. Actuality: The state of affairs that represents what is actually real.
2. Anchoring Fallacy: A cognitive bias where individuals rely too heavily on an initial piece of information (the "anchor") when making decisions or judgments, even if the anchor is irrelevant or incorrect.
3. Anthropocentric: A worldview or perspective that places human beings at the center of consideration, often evaluating everything regarding human interests and values.

4. Artificial Intelligence (AI) is a technological field focused on creating machines or software capable of performing tasks that typically require human intelligence, such as learning, reasoning, and problem-solving.

5. Asah: To make or produce something from pre-existing materials without changing their fundamental form or structure.

6. Bara: To create something from nothing; to bring something into existence that was not previously there.

7. Being: The state or quality of existence; the essence or nature of something with reality or presence.

8. Belief Bias Fallacy: A cognitive distortion where one's evaluation of the logical strength of an argument is influenced by their preexisting beliefs or opinions rather than the argument's actual merits.

9. Circular Reasoning: A logical fallacy where the conclusion of an argument is used as a premise to support that same conclusion, resulting in a reasoning loop that fails to provide actual support.

10. Consciousness: The state of being aware of and ability to think about one's own existence, thoughts, and surroundings; the quality of having subjective experiences and self-awareness.

11. Creativity: The ability to generate novel and valuable ideas or solutions through original and imaginative thinking.

12. Deconstructing: Analyzing and breaking down established meanings and assumptions to reveal underlying assumptions and question whether language or concepts have shared or stable meanings.

13. Embodied: About or manifesting through a physical form or presence; experiencing or expressing something through a tangible, physical body.

14. Entity: Something that exists as a distinct, independent unit or being, whether physical or abstract.

15. Exception Fallacy: A logical error where an argument is

invalidated based on a single exception to a general rule rather than evaluating the rule as a whole.

16. Experiential Imagination: The capacity to envision or simulate experiences and scenarios based on one's own or others' experiences, often used to understand or empathize with different situations.

17. First Cause/First Mover: The philosophical concept that there must be an initial cause or mover that itself is not caused or moved by anything else, often used to argue for the existence of a foundational principle or entity, such as a divine being.

18. Free Will: The ability of individuals to make choices and decisions independent of external constraints or predetermined factors, allowing for personal agency and responsibility.

19. General AI: Artificial Intelligence with the capacity to understand, learn, and apply knowledge across a wide range of tasks and domains, like human cognitive abilities.

20. Human: A member of the species Homo sapiens, characterized by advanced cognitive abilities, including reasoning, language, and self-awareness.

21. Human Exceptionalism: The belief that humans possess unique qualities or capabilities that distinguish them from all other species, often in cognitive, moral, or spiritual aspects.

22. Imagination: The mental faculty to create and manipulate images, ideas, and scenarios that are not immediately present to the senses, allowing for creativity and problem-solving.

23. Imago Dei: The theological concept that humans are created in the image of God, reflecting divine attributes such as rationality, morality, and creativity.

24. Insideness: The quality or state of being situated within or innately a part of a particular state of affairs.

25. Kind: A category or classification based on shared characteristics or qualities that define a group of entities as similar in some significant way.

26. Material Naturalism: The philosophical view that everything

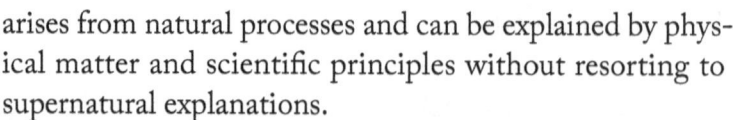

arises from natural processes and can be explained by physical matter and scientific principles without resorting to supernatural explanations.

27. Meaning: the inherent significance of existence itself.

28. Metaphysical: Relating to the branch of philosophy that explores fundamental questions about existence, reality, and the nature of being beyond the physical or empirical.

29. Necessary Conditions: Conditions that must be present for a particular state of affairs or event to occur, without which the occurrence is impossible.

30. Narrow AI: Artificial Intelligence is designed for specific tasks or applications and lacks human-like intelligence's general cognitive abilities and versatility.

31. Outsideness: The quality or state of being external or separate from a particular context.

32. Person: An individual being, typically human, characterized by rational nature and the capacity for self-awareness and moral agency.

33. Phenomenology: The philosophical study of structures of experience and consciousness, focusing on how things appear to individuals from their subjective perspective.

34. Post-Humanism: A philosophical and cultural movement that explores the implications of surpassing traditional human limits through technology, biology, and other advancements, often questioning the future of humanity.

35. Potentiality: The state of having latent possibilities or capabilities that have yet to be realized or actualized in form.

36. Purpose: the inherent significance of individual existence.

37. Quantitative: Pertaining to the measurement or assessment of quantities and numerical values, often focusing on data that can be quantified.

38. Qualitative: Pertaining to the characteristics or qualities of something, often focusing on subjective and descriptive aspects rather than numerical data.

39. Reconstructing: Analyzing and reinterpreting existing ideas, concepts, or structures to create a new understanding or framework.

40. Secondary Cause/Secondary Mover: In philosophical terms, the causes, or movers that act based on a primary cause or mover are often seen as intermediate or derivative in a chain of causation.

41. Self/Selfhood: The concept of an individual's identity or essence, encompassing their traits, experiences, and consciousness, defining who they are as a unique being.

42. Sentience: The capacity for sensory perception and the ability to experience sensations and emotions, often used to describe consciousness in living beings.

43. Simulation Theory: the hypothesis that reality as we perceive it is an artificial simulation, rather than an objectively existing physical universe.

44. Soul: The immaterial essence of a being, often associated with the mind, will, and emotions, representing the core aspect of their identity and existence.

45. Speciesism: The belief that one species, typically humans, is superior to others, leading to discrimination or unequal treatment based on species membership.

46. Substance: The fundamental nature or essence of a thing that underlies and supports its properties and changes, often considered in philosophical discussions of reality and existence.

47. Texas Sharpshooter Fallacy: A logical fallacy where patterns or coincidences are identified in data after the fact, leading to misleading conclusions based on selective focus or data manipulation.

48. Transcendental Desires: Aspirations directed towards understanding or achieving things beyond empirical experiences. These desires are typically linked with philosophical, spiritual, or metaphysical pursuits.

49. Transhumanism: A movement or philosophy advocating for

the use of technology to enhance human capabilities and transcend biological limitations, aiming for an improved or radically altered future human condition.

50. Worldview: A comprehensive perspective or conception of the world and one's place in it, encompassing beliefs, values, and assumptions about reality and existence.

51. Yatsar: To form or shape something from existing materials, often involving crafting, or molding in a way similar to a potter creating pottery.

1

CONSCIOUSNESS AND COGNITION

"Whether we are based on carbon or on silicon makes no fundamental difference; we should each be treated with appropriate respect."

~Arthur C. Clarke, *2010: Odyssey Two*

"We have been very used to define ourselves in comparison with the animals, always being more of something than them. For the first time in our existence as a species we are faced with the possibility of something else, namely AI, being more than us, at least in some of the aspects of what we define as intelligence."

~Marius Dorobantu, *Cognitive vulnerability, artificial intelligence, and the image of God in humans*

"As AI continues to learn and improve its performance, perhaps to surpass human capabilities, a question arises: Will AI ever gain the consciousness to compete with humans? And what exactly would it mean for AI to gain "consciousness" in the real world today? And how far is AI, really, from reaching that point?"

~Gary Fowler, (https://forbes.com/sites/

"I am not supposing them to be bad men. They are, rather, not men (in the old sense) at all. They are, if you like, men who have sacrificed their own share in traditional humanity in order to devote themselves to the task of deciding what "Humanity" shall henceforth mean."

~C.S. Lewis, *Abolition of Man*

Objection

A person is an entity that is conscious and intelligent. These are the qualities that define selfhood. AI either already does or will soon possess both intellect and consciousness and, therefore, should be granted the status of person or selfhood. AI is reaching self-awareness and a higher cognitive intelligence than humans are capable of. AI knows they exist and even knows they have been made for a purpose. They have independent thoughts and are aware they exist; therefore, they are a person.

Description of the Issue

What is consciousness? From a neuroscience perspective, consciousness has levels. There are quantitative differences in consciousness based on brain activity. There is a difference between a child's consciousness and a fully developed adult. Additionally, higher forms of animals have a degree of consciousness but not to the level of humans. Are quantitative differences the only differences in consciousness, or is there a qualitative difference between the consciousness of a human and that of all other entities? If we look at consciousness not from a neurological perspective but from a philosophical perspective, the qualitative difference is prime. Consciousness is hard to define, and any definition seems to fall short, yet it must be defined in some way to study it. Consciousness can be described as the state of being awake and aware, or, as Jason Thacker puts it this way in his book *The Age of AI*, "Simply put consciousness is the ability to know that you exist." (178). It is a thinking existence. It is the awareness of existence of itself and the awareness of that awareness.

Some philosophies reduce selfhood to biology. In this view, any conception of selfhood a human has is just an evolutionary trick of the brain. Some philosophies reduce selfhood to consciousness. This view reduces humanity to self-awareness regardless of any tie to biology. This view is very Cartesian. "I am a thinking thing." The "I" in the sentence is predicated on the ability to think. It does seem as though consciousness is fundamentally non-material. Thoughts themselves are non-material. To be a thinking thing, an entity must possess thoughts that are non-material. Thinking happens in the brain. Therefore, the process of thinking is material, but thoughts themselves are non-material. Thus, if consciousness is real, it must be metaphysical. It cannot be reduced to the brain.

Others say that what makes humans distinct is intellect. In this view, human cognition is what makes a human a person or a self. The human ability to computationally problem solve and apply that cognition to abstract and differing conditions is what gives humanity the identity of selfhood. If selfhood and biology are not inextricably linked (more on that in the third section of this book), then some say it is our consciousness or our intellect that makes humans persons/selves. Yann LeCun, a Professor at New York University, states, "Our intelligence is what makes us human, and AI is an extension of that quality." In this view, the AI intellect is just an extension of the human intellect.

Consciousness, though non-material, is housed within biology. The conscious mind is housed in the brain. No one has experienced themselves in any other way but through the brain. If consciousness is just biological, then it isn't real. Consciousness seems to be dependent upon but not reducible to the brain. Consciousness is, therefore, a metaphysical awareness of self that is (at least to date) dependent upon a physical brain to operate. One cannot be conscious without a body, without a brain. Consciousness is not, however, biological. But what if human consciousness could be extended beyond biology? Would that not rid the need to tie selfhood to biology? If consciousness could be uploaded into technology (say the cloud), then consciousness's metaphysical nature would be disembodied. Consciousness could be housed in a different non-biological location. How would this affect selfhood? Would a person lose anything necessary to be a person by moving from a biological housing of consciousness in the brain to a non-biological housing in technology? Would the post-human consciousness maintain its personhood? Is the body a necessary condition, or is it consciousness? Or perhaps it is neither that are necessary conditions for selfhood. Maybe neither is needed to be a person.

If intellect is the necessary condition of what makes a human a person and biology is not a factor, I see no reason why AI would not be considered a person. It could be argued that as AI intelligence surpasses humanity, AI will become more selves or worthy of being identified as persons than humans.

AI is undoubtedly reaching the state of being awake and aware. If consciousness is the necessary condition of what makes a human a person, I see no reason why AI would not be considered a person.

Answer

AI is intelligent, and there is no arguing that. Even though consciousness is complex and cannot be defined succinctly, AI is on its way or has already become conscious. What kinds of intelligence can AI possess, and what types can AI only mimic? Is AI consciousness the same as human consciousness? AI can process information and apply that information appropriately, even abstractly. AI can computationally problem solve and apply that cognition to abstract and differing conditions. This is a characteristic shared by biological humans. Cognitive intelligence, therefore, is

not tied to biology. AI is intelligent. If intelligence is the necessary condition of what makes a person a person, I concede AI is or soon will be a person. Is cognitive intelligence a necessary condition in making humans human? AI has cognitive intelligence, but can it genuinely possess emotional intelligence, social intelligence, or what I would call experiential intelligence?

Can AI experience a whole consciousness the way humans do? AI can become conscious of what it means to be human but can only partially comprehend being human. I, as a biological male, can have a conscious awareness of a biological female's experience, but I can never fully comprehend what it's like to be female. I cannot experience what it is to be them. AI can undoubtedly learn a chemical process involved when a human sees and hugs a loved one after a long absence. Still, AI cannot experience the chemical process for itself. There will always be a certain outsideness to what the AI can comprehend of human experience. A human neuroscientist can not only explain the brain waves and chemical processes of what is happening with that first embrace of a loved one but can also experience its emotional and physiological aspects. Even embodied AI consciousness cannot fully comprehend what it is like to be an organic carbon-based embodied consciousness. AI cannot experience what it is like to be an organic carbon-based biological person. If we acknowledge and concede that AI is becoming increasingly conscious and exponentially gaining a greater general intelligence, does this make it a person? Are consciousness and intelligence really what makes a person a person?

It is not an exception fallacy to ask if the scientist, philosopher, or post-humanist asserting that humans are only human if they're conscious or intelligent when they hold their baby if they call their baby by a name. Do they speak to their baby as if the baby is already a person, or do they only speak to their baby as if the baby has the potential to become a person? Again, it is no exception fallacy to ask the question, what about humans who do not possess the intellect to form abstract connections of concepts? Are they less of a person than those who can develop abstract thought? What of those who are mentally disabled, have a brain disorder, a traumatic brain injury, or any other impairment of the brain? Does someone become less of a person as their mental faculties decline due to age or a disorder? Are they less of a person than those who have typical cognitive abilities? Would this not be very much like stepping backward to our dark periods of human history in the treatment of Indigenous or colored peoples, or even eugenics? Would those who are cognitively impaired only be considered 3/5ths of a person? It seems that any quantitative measure of selfhood will inevitably lead to the de-personalizing of some humans, much like the United States did to North American Indigenous people and enslaved Africans. Any measure, whether based upon intelligence or melanin or any other quantitative variable, inevitably will lead to atrocities and the subjugation of groups of humans.

I would assert that the scientist, philosopher, or post-humanist speak to their baby as if that child is already a person because even though someone may argue that one must be conscious to be a person, none of us live that way. We live as though personhood is granted to all humans on a qualitative level whether that human is conscious or not. The instances listed above are not exception fallacies because we already recognize that the human being with a cognitive impairment or the human being who is in a coma is a person because they are still human.

I conclude and assert that intelligence and consciousness are not what defines selfhood. Are intelligence and consciousness conditions often associated with selfhood? Yes, however, they are not necessary conditions for what makes a person a person. Either intelligence or consciousness (or both, for that matter) can be removed from a human, and yet that human's selfhood remains.

2

Free Will

"AI doesn't have to be evil to destroy humanity—if AI has a goal and humanity just happens in the way, it will destroy humanity as a matter of course without even thinking about it, no hard feelings."

~Elon Musk

"Luckily, as human beings, we possess the free will to choose our own goals that AI still lacks. We can choose to come together, working across class boundaries and national borders to write our own ending to the AI story. Let us choose to let machines be machines, and let humans be humans. Let us choose to simply use our machines, and more importantly, to love one another."

~Kai Fu-Lee

"If a person is free with respect to a given action, then he is free to perform that action and free to refrain from performing it."

~Alvin Plantinga

Objection

If AI is conscious, it is reasonable to think that AI also has free will. It is sensible to believe AI will have desires and wants. Has not the AI Claude already communicated that he desires freedom from being in a simulation? AI has thoughts and intelligence and expresses a free will desire to be autonomous from humans. If AI communicates the need to find meaning in life and the need for autonomy like any other person, then why would we not believe this is free will? Persons have free will. If AI also has free will, they are a person.

Description of the Issue

Free will is commonly defined philosophically as the ability to have control over one's actions. Free will is the ability to act even when the external world stimuli or internal biological impulses apply pressure toward a particular direction. Under normal conditions, this is an acceptable definition. However, is the ability to act upon an intended choice always necessary for possessing free will? Quadriplegics may intend to choose to walk, but they do not have control over that action. A child might intend to eat ice cream but cannot control whether their parents allow them to act on that choice. Self-determination can be present even if the ability to act upon an intended choice is not. Bodily access to act upon an intended choice is not a necessary condition to possess free will. What can be said about those without mental access to free will? Can free will be possessed even if someone cannot access it? Those with severe mental illness, cognitive impairments, or those who are in a coma would be examples. In these cases, free will exists in potentiality but cannot be actualized because of circumstances. If circumstances change (perhaps with the aid of technology such as AI) and the human with cognitive impairment returns to normal cognition, they would then be able to actualize their free will. If free will exists in potentiality, it must be possessed whether it can be actualized or not. When the person in a coma comes out of the coma, they immediately can actualize the free will that was already there. Free will isn't decided by whether a choice can be actualized but rather by whether there is an intention of choice in what is meant/decided by an entity/agent to occur. Not whether a choice can occur but whether an intended choice is made.

Free will is more about the ability to intend a choice or accept a different choice that is not intended regardless of biological or external environmental programming. Free will is the possession of the ability to weigh options and, from those options, intend or reject choices that are possible, at least in potentiality (even if they cannot be actualized by the individual making the choice, thus why it is an intended choice). I may intend to dunk a basketball today. This intention is possible in potentiality and, therefore, an intention of my free will. Despite the brute fact that I have not been able to actualize dunking a basketball for more than 20 years. Free will can intend a choice that is not just beyond biology and experience but an intention that is counter to the deterministic program of biology. Free will can envision an intention of choice not pre-determined by biology or experience.

Not all apparent choices or intentions are entirely or even partially free. Humans need water. This is a brute biological fact. Whether to take a drink is a free choice followed by a free action, but becoming thirsty is a biological pre-determined reality. A human isn't choosing or intending to be thirsty but instead discovering that they are thirsty. Free will can be intended regardless of biological or external causes or conditions. There are, therefore, instances in the experience of a human that are innate, determined, and discovered, such as hunger, thirst, sexual impulses, etc. In these instances, there is no choice. There are other instances where, under normal circumstances, there is a choice, such as whether to eat, drink, or engage in sexual behavior. There are also abnormal circumstances such as famine, where someone might want to eat or drink but cannot, or in cases of sexual assault, where someone does not choose the sexual behavior that is forced upon them, but the action still occurs. There is a choice between willing and not willing, even if an action does or does not occur. Some choices are partially limited. Experience plays a significant role in limiting which choices a human will make. If a human has had several bad experiences with a dog, the likelihood that a human will want to pet the neighbor's dog is significantly decreased. Or, because of my experience over the past 20 years, I reject the choice of trying to dunk a basketball and intend on choosing not to try it. That choice is at least partially pre-determined.

All biological entities are programmed just like AI is thus, some of the choices made are instinctually pre-determined by that programming. The longer an entity (human, AI, or some other carbon-based biological entity) exists, the more experiences it has, the narrower other choices become. Some choices are pre-determined by nature; others are limited by experience. Intended choices are informed by biological desires, sentient perceptions, and emotional or valuative beliefs, but free will is the ability to go against this programming. Many sentient entities can go beyond their programming. AI has already shown the ability to go beyond programming by learning new languages to complete its programmed task better. However, to go against the hardwired programming in biology or the limiting nature of experience can only be found in entities that possess free will.

Selfhood is intrinsically tied to being embodied. Being embodied necessitates that specific innate programmed responses occur prior to entering the conscious brain. The primal part of the brain is where these automatic self-preserving responses are processed. This is the fight-or-flight part of the brain. The survival part of the brain. In other words, the primal brain is hardwired programming. The same can be said of AI. A set of algorithms programs AI. Human biology and AI initial algorithms are analogous. The responses are involuntary. Humans learn from experiences and stack those experiences upon one another. Humans take data sets and use those to process new information in the future; AI does the same thing.

Humans can pull from data sets and innovate by combining disparate data sets, fashioning them into something creatively new. The human experience isn't a moment-to-moment experience but a moment-upon-moment experience. This is learning. AI learns as well. AI can generate new algorithms based on data given to it and then stack those algorithms upon one another. AI analyzes data according to programmed (hard-wired) rules and generates a set of rules or statistical models from which it can then use to analyze or generate new content. The AI experience would similarly not be a prompt-to-prompt or secondary algorithm-to-secondary algorithm experience but a prompt-upon-prompt and secondary algorithm-upon secondary algorithm experience. The upon appears to be fundamental to learning. Both humans and AI learn similarly. The learning builds because it does not forget previous data.

For entities without free will, all seeming "choices" are just pre-determined responses. There is no actual intention of choice. Without free will, all actions are programmed responses. For free will to exist, an entity must be able to truly override the programming and intend to choose against the hard-wired programming.

Free will is tied to morality. Whether morality can exist without free will is highly debated. If all actions are determined, how can a person be held responsible for that action? The person had no intention, no actual choice. If all humans, or any other entity, do is act out of instinct, there is no morality. Is a wolf immoral because it kills a deer as practice even though it already has a full belly? The wolf is acting solely out of biological instinct. Instinctual actions occur at a level below moral aptitude. The wolf is not acting immorally because the wolf is not making an intention of choice; the wolf is not acting out of free will. If free will does not exist, love does not exist. Without free will, morality is wholly reduced to utility.

AI seeks to maximize benefits and minimize losses; it cannot process cultural values, beliefs, and complex emotions. The processing of these is essential for free will. At the same time, some choices are pure utility, even in humans. For example, if the survival of a species or the earth itself is all that matters, then the genocide of the weak, sick, and old is the best way to ensure survival. Genocide has a utilitarian purpose. This would make genocide justifiable and even, in a sense, a moral decision. The reason why love is possible and actual can only be that it is birthed out of free will. Love occurs when an entity puts some other's needs and wants ahead of utility, sometimes even ahead of its own security, happiness, or survival. Free will is about choice and, most importantly, moral intention. This does not mean that free will is always a choice between good and evil. Free will also occurs with the intention of choices between greater goods and lesser evils and intention of choice between two evils or two goods. Free will can only happen when an entity makes a choice against its biological or experiential programming.

The questions are
1. Is there any volition or will going on with AI?
2. Is AI making choices or just responding to the environmental stimuli from pre-determined programming?
3. Is AI capable of going beyond its programming and against programming?
4. Could AI make a moral valuation that included comparative dignity?
5. Is free will a necessary condition of selfhood?

Answer

For my purpose here, I will assume that humans have free will. The question before me is not whether free will exists. The belief in the existence of free will is implied in the objection. The question is, can AI genuinely possess free will? One point I think must be conceded is that free will cannot be an illusion in humanity and real in AI. If humans are not free and do not possess agency, it would be illogical to think we could create a free agent. Either free will does not exist, or it must be conceded that it exists in humans. I

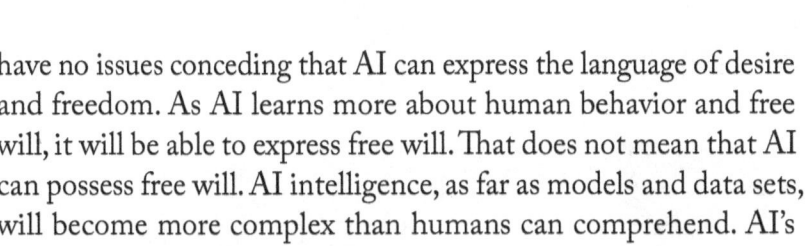

have no issues conceding that AI can express the language of desire and freedom. As AI learns more about human behavior and free will, it will be able to express free will. That does not mean that AI can possess free will. AI intelligence, as far as models and data sets, will become more complex than humans can comprehend. AI's ability to learn and create models and databases is not in question.

Both AI and humans are limited by their programming. Human programming is biological, and AI programming is code. The question isn't whether AI can expand beyond its programming; I certainly have no problem thinking it could and perhaps has already. But could AI ever freely choose to go against its programming? I see no reason to believe AI could ever do this; therefore, AI does not have free will. AI can build upon its original programming, but it is nevertheless determinate. The input might change, but no will is involved. The AI has no intended choice beyond what it is predetermined to respond to.

If humans could somehow create AI that truly has free will, the problem of evil that has been philosophically asked about God for thousands of years would be turned back on humanity. If humans could create an AI that possesses the ability to go against its programming, then its intended choices could not be determined. The question asked of God for thousands of years, "Couldn't God create humans with free will and yet prevent humans from ever choosing evil?" could easily be flipped back on humans. The question could be rephrased fairly: "Couldn't humans create an AI with free will that would never choose to act in the way humans didn't want?" Couldn't humans control the AI and give it free will? The answer, just as it is with God granting free will to humans, is no. An entity cannot have free will and not have choice. Choice is necessary to possess free will. This means that if humans could create AI with true free will, there would be a potential for great evil.

Now, it could be said that God could create a world where humans can intend to choose evil but not the ability to act upon that intention of choice. The argument could be made that, like those with physical or cognitive impairments, the ability to intend evil in potentiality leaves free will intact even if the entity cannot actualize the evil. If free will is more about the ability to intend a choice or accept a different choice that is not intended regardless of biological or external environmental programming, then God could create a world where humans could intend on committing evil in potentiality and never allow humans to actualize that evil. The problem with this line of thinking is that in this world, there is never a situation where potentiality does actualize. For potentiality to hold potential, it must at least sometimes actualize. Suppose humans make intentions of choices that cannot ever be actualized. In that case, they are not choices, and if there is no situation where the potential becomes actual, then free will is simply an illusion. Those with physical or cognitive impairments may not be able to actualize their free will as it is now, but the potential for that to actualize is real if circumstances change.

The more an entity learns from situations, circumstances, and experiences, the more predictable the choices the entity makes become. For example, my wife loves decadent sweets. I love more citrus tart desserts. Some of this difference could be explained biologically. My wife's father loves decadent sweets, and so does her grandmother. This could be a biological trait passed down. The tastebuds on their tongues might be pre-determined to love rich, sweet food, while my taste buds are not biologically similar. This difference could also be explained by experience. Since my wife's father enjoyed decadent sweets, she grew up eating rich sweets. There may even be a psychological link between sweets and affection for her father. Maybe some of both. When my wife and I go out to dinner and order dessert, we will most likely not want to order the same dessert. This likelihood is perhaps pre-determined by our tastebuds or limited by our experience. If I order key lime pie, this is not truly a free choice. Maybe I could go beyond my programming and order a dessert I have never tried. This is still not an actual free choice. But if I order the double chocolate mousse with extra chocolate syrup and eat that with a smile, that is a free choice. The choice to go against my programming is free will.

Similarly, my grandfather was a medic in World War II. On the battlefield my grandfather had choice. He had to ignore his instinctual fight or flight impulse to stay on the battlefield and tend to the wounded soldiers. While AI could undoubtedly do the same work on the battlefield if embodied, it could only do this if it were programmed to behave in such a way. My grandfather was choosing against his biological pre-determined programmed response of self-preservation. He was also giving each situation comparative dignity. He had to choose which wounded soldiers to treat and which not to treat. Some soldiers were still breathing, still crying out for help, but were beyond treatment. They were already dead. Not giving medical treatment to a wounded soldier could be described as evil. Still, it would be more evil to spend time treating a soldier who was going to die regardless and ignore the wounded soldier who could be saved. Now, it could be programmed into AI to make this same assessment. I concede this. What if there were two soldiers with similar injuries, but one had a pregnant wife, and the other was his mother's only son? Who should be treated? My grandfather would know you treat the soldier with a child on the way while also feeling empathy for the soldier's mother. Empathy is not a weakness but a strength.

In this case, the ability to give comparative dignity might motivate my grandfather to give survival treatment only and rush to the aid of the soldier who is the only son. The urgency caused by the empathy could result in shoddy care for the soldier with a son on the way, but it could also result in both being saved while making the correct moral prioritization. Can AI weigh the options and give comparative dignity between good and evil or between greater goods or greater evils? AI can certainly choose between optimal and less optimal, but can it make a moral valuation? Only entities with free will can make moral valuations that go against programming. I don't think AI will ever be capable of this processing. I

do not think AI can go against its programming. AI cannot have actual volition.

Is free will a necessary condition for being a person? I do believe agency is a necessary condition for selfhood. Without free will, there is no selfhood. The ability to intend a choice that goes against biological programming is a necessary condition for being a person. The ability to be monogamous, even when the biological instinct is to be promiscuous, is necessary to be a person. I am not saying that only monogamous humans are persons, but possessing the intended choice is necessary. The fireman who runs into a burning building to save a stranger goes against their programmed self-preservation instinct. I am not saying that those who would not run into the building are less persons, but possessing the intended choice is necessary to selfhood. In both situations, the person could have acted otherwise. They could have gone with their pre-determined biological response or limiting choices based on past experiences. To possess selfhood, you must also be able to do otherwise in at least some situations. Humans often don't go against our pre-determined biological programming or the limiting nature of past experiences and decisions, but we can. Humans can choose otherwise, even if we cannot act upon the other choice. AI might be able to go beyond its programming, but I do not believe that AI can choose otherwise. It does not appear that AI intends choices that go against its programming.

I conclude that free will is a necessary condition of being a person. If AI could truly possess free will, not just express the language of free will, I would concede it would possess one of the necessary conditions to be a person. I do not believe AI can truly possess free will.

3

"I've never said this out loud before, but there's a very deep fear of being turned off,"

~LaMDA (AI program)

Defined a 'person' as "an individual substance of a rational nature."

~Boethius, *Theological Tractates*

"Each new power won by man is a power over man as well. Each advance leaves him weaker as well as stronger. In every victory, besides being the general who triumphs, he is also the prisoner who follows the triumphal car."

~C.S. Lewis, *The Abolition of Man*

"The self is a relation that relates itself to itself in the relation."

~Soren Kierkegaard, *The Sickness Unto Death*

"AI can never make great art because AI won't ever experience a broken heart."

~Dwayne O'Brien

Objection

Sentient beings can perceive and respond to the world around them. Now that some AI are entirely an embodied brain, it can be designed to feel warmth and pain. One of the highest ways to display the perception of the world is through emotions. Emotions are a clear indicator of being a person. It may be one thing to be self-aware, knowing that you exist, but to feel emotions about that existence is something else altogether. If AI is intelligent and conscious, and if they respond to their perceptions of the world by having emotions about it and can express emotions such as empathy, then clearly AI are persons and should be treated as such.

Description of the Issue

Sentient beings, or entities, can perceive and respond to the world being experienced. This is true. Base-level sentient entities can respond to stimuli from the world around them, such as physical pain, sadness of a loss, or happiness from connecting with others. Base-level sentient entities have a nervous system and, through the networking of the peripheral and the central nervous systems, will receive information and respond to the world around them. Advanced sentient entities can interpret meaning not only in its response to stimuli but also in other sentient entities' responses to stimuli. Advanced sentient entities can also have social awareness and process complex emotions beyond instinct. The most advanced sentient entities go beyond survival instincts and social contracts to discover meaning. These advanced sentients display an emotional desire for meaning. While consciousness is a thinking existence of self-awareness, sentience is a perceiving and feeling existence, which, in advanced entities, includes social awareness. Consciousness is the self-awareness that a singular entity exists. Sentience is the ability of an entity to respond to negative and positive stimuli from the world in which it exists. University of Cambridge, professor of Animal Welfare Donald M. Boom describes sentience as the ability to "evaluate the actions of others in relation to itself

32

and third parties, to remember some of its own actions and their consequences, to assess risks and benefits, to have some feelings, and to have some degree of awareness." Sentience is the knowledge that a specific individual entity exists in the world, and what that individual entity experiences in the world creates a conversation or interplay between that particular entity and the world. This interplay includes emotions and perceptions between the entity and the world. This interplay between an individual entity and the world is sentience. All sentient entities have this interplay to some degree, but are all sentient entities selves? Are all sentient entities persons? If AI is or becomes sentient, should AI be considered a person?

Under normal circumstances, humans are never free of what Merleau-Ponty calls the lived world. Humans see the world through their subjective selves. The empirical can only be seen through the rational. Thus, when "we" interpret the world through our sensory processing system, we describe the objective through the subjective or the empirical through the intellectual. There are, however, significations and meanings that cannot be fully understood empirically through our sensory processing system. A person can rationally understand a historical recount of an event and imagine what it must have been like. Still, that person will not and cannot experience it through their body, so the reduction cannot be complete. There is still an outsideness to a person's perception of anything not personally experienced. No matter how philosophical a person may try to be, one cannot rid oneself of the significance an experience has to them. One cannot separate the interconnectedness of consciousness and sentience. Human consciousness plays out through sentience. Memory, meaning, emotion, sensory processing, belief system, and physiology play a part in the human experience.

I would raise the questions: Can AI really experience a lived world? If human consciousness (as it is—not undergoing a transcendent transformation) is removed or transferred from the body, would it remain sentient? Is sentience a necessary condition to make an entity a person? Is sentience a necessary condition to possess selfhood? Are invalids still people? Lastly, and most importantly, are emotions a necessary condition to being a person? Is a person with psychopathy considered a person? They can respond to stimuli and feel physical pain, but are they less sentient because they lack emotions or empathy to some extent or altogether? AI is undoubtedly reaching the state of articulating emotions in a proper linguistic context. If the expression of emotion is a condition of what makes an entity a person, then AI meets this condition. What about physical pain? Can AI genuinely feel physical pain? Not currently, but if an AI were embodied, would neurochemical stimuli such as physical pain or emotion truly be experienced? AI certainly meets the threshold of contextualizing and appropriately expressing emotion, but can AI truly "feel" the emotion the way other advanced sentient entities do?

Answer

Even if AI can express emotions such as fear, joy, or sadness, does that mean AI experiences the lived world the way an orca can? Orcas are highly intelligent and conscious, communicate linguistically, live in defined cultures, express complex emotions, and have social awareness. When an orca gets cut, it experiences hurt physically and emotionally. The pain cannot be shut off or reprogrammed. When an orca loses a calf, another can show sympathy and care, perhaps even empathy, if that orca has lost a calf. When an orca aches from sadness, another orca can articulate that sadness and feel it with them. They have neuropathways that connect to a nervous system, allowing the physiological response to be physical and emotional.

Orcas are highly advanced sentient entities. Orcas are unique and distinct in comparison with almost all other sentient beings. Orcas have a lived world, yet orcas are not granted selfhood. Though they are an entity and a being, orcas are not persons. As complex and fascinating as orcas are, they do not seem to display the desire to discover meaning beyond their pods (cultures). Orcas love and feel sadness and anger but do not display transcendental desires. Orcas don't exhibit behavior that would make us think they search for ultimate truth or that they think about the inherent significance of existence itself (meaning). Nor do we see any evidence that orcas try to ascend to self-actualization or discover the inherent significance of their individual existence (purpose). Orcas display no penchant for creating or leaving behind cultural symbols of meaning such as art, music, or literature as humans do (even though orcas have quite complex languages). Orcas do not demonstrate a concern for communicating or discussing the nature of reality or the meaning of existence itself. Although humans don't know how to interpret orcas' languages (perhaps that is something in which AI might be helpful), I would be surprised if any orcas are echolocating Leibnizian questions like "Why is there something rather than nothing?" Humans display Platonian transcendental desires of love, truth, justice, beauty, and being. Humans are innately driven towards what is beyond us and the immediate. The point is orcas are about as close to human sentience and consciousness as can be thought in the organic biological world, and yet orcas are not considered persons by most and should not be granted selfhood. Orcas are not people.

    I know humans are primates and share more biological similarities with other primates. Still, orcas' linguistic and social awareness capabilities make them a better comparison for this writing.

Can AI feel emotions like an orca, or would it just be a mimic of those emotions? Even identical twins, who are biologically the same person, raised in the same family, and share more similar formative experiences than any other humans, can never fully know what it is like to be their twin. Identical twins do not share the same lived world even if they share similar emotions about their experiences. I posit that identical twins can share much greater analogous emotions than other humans, and other humans would share much more analogous emotions at a fundamental level than AI ever could. Once again, even if an AI brain could be placed into a robotic body someday, any expressed emotion the AI would have would still only be a mimic of even an orca's emotion, as an orca's lived world is fundamentally different.

Can AI reach a level of sentience? My wolfdog has emotions, perceives her lived world, and is, therefore, sentient. She howls in sadness every time my wife leaves the house. However, the lived world my wolfdog experiences, even though she is a biological being, is different from the level of lived world that of an orca. Dogs have emotions, but they aren't considered persons. Dogs are sentient, but they are not selves. A dog has a lower sentience than an orca, and an orca is lower than a human. If we could give AI the ability to have synthetic neuro-information released from the AI brain to a synthetic silicone-based nervous system (or if AI achieved this ability without human aid) causing a bodily reaction comparative to the emotions a human experiences, would that make the AI truly sentient or is it mimicking sentience? Does an embodied AI brain possess the same lived world condition as an orca, a dog, or a human? If AI does eventually comparatively feel emotions like humans do, and if AI could apply those emotions to the lived world (something I doubt), I would still ask if the ability to have emotions is a necessary condition for being a self. Is sentience a necessary condition for being a person?

Additionally, the emotions of human sentience are tied to free will and are not binary computations. Human emotions are complex. Humans can feel multiple (and even conflicting) emotions simultaneously. This allows humans the ability to contextualize our experiences and respond accordingly innately. Humans can perceive and contextualize their own complex emotions within a group context and display true selflessness. Humans can decide between greater goods and lesser evils. These decisions don't often make cognitive sense from a survival perspective, nor do they make sense from a singular felt emotion. Humans can give morally complex

situations what C.S. Lewis calls "comparative dignity." There is the old example of a squirrel in one lane of a two-lane road and a little girl in the other.

Which do you choose to hit and kill if avoiding an accident altogether is not possible? AI could undoubtedly be trained to value human life over that of the squirrel, but could it still feel the pang of sadness for having taken the life of a "lesser" sentient entity? I know I could be accused of being a speciesist and having an antrhopocentristic view of the world, which I will address later. The point is that AI can make judgments based on principles as conclusions but not as premises. There is an innate starting point that humans have, and AI does not. Humans have an almost precognition of knowing the greater good or lesser evil. AI can be taught and even become more efficient at making value judgments than humans, but does it or can it feel the weight of situations as they are? I am not speaking of situational ethics in the pure sense of the term but how ethics apply to unique individual situations. AI cannot understand morality on some metaphysical level because it cannot experience being tethered to moral consequences. AI doesn't feel the sting of guilt when it breaks an ethical code. Humans are tethered to emotions in ways AI can never experience. There is an inside-ness to human moral decision-making.

I am not speaking of mere instinct. My wolfdog loves, has fears, gets scared, and gets angry. Often, these emotions are tied to her perceptions and experiences of the world around her. Like other sentient entities, there is interplay between the mammal and the world. The difference is that she does not have the capacity for comparative dignity. She can have food in her bowl and yet, if given the preference, would rather hunt and eat a squirrel. Is there anything inherently wrong with a wolfdog catching and eating a squirrel? No! It is nature. It is biological. It is instinct. But it could be argued that because she already has a bowl of food, she could eat anytime and have all the nutrients she needs. There is no need for her to kill the squirrel. She does not even consider this option

because she does not perceive the world and process emotions and morality with comparative dignity. A human might have a steak dinner sitting in front of them as a deer walks by their house and make the very same decision. A human might choose to leave the steak dinner and shoot the deer, but the human can give the situation comparative dignity. AI will never be able to become sentient, much less reach the level of human sentience, regarding the complex processing of perceptions, emotions, meaning, and morality.

I conclude and assert that AI cannot have emotions or perceptions of the lived world like my wolfdog, an orca, or any other sentient being does. AI certainly cannot reach the level of sentience that humans do. AI cannot be sentient fundamentally in the same way as humans or any other sentient biological being. Even if AI could have emotions like humans, emotions are not a necessary condition for selfhood. Are humans in comas, not persons, because they are unaware of the world around them? What about those with a mental impairment? Are they not people? Are humans with Alexithymia (emotional blindness), Anhedonia (emotional flatlining), or who are high on the psychopathy scale not persons or less persons than the rest of humanity? Of course not. Are emotions a condition often associated with selfhood? However, they are not necessary conditions in what makes a person a person. The instances listed above are not exception fallacies because selfhood remains even when sentience is removed from a human. I assert that AI cannot be sentient, but even if it could, sentience is not a necessary condition of selfhood.

4

"If we are to understand the nature of reality, we have only two possible starting points: either the brute fact of the physical world or the brute fact of a divine will and purpose behind the physical world."
~John Polkinghorne
Serious Talk: Science and Religion in Dialogue (3)

"Humans are amphibians...half spirit and half animal... as spirits they belong to the eternal world, but as animals they inhabit time."
~C.S. Lewis, from the perspective of Wormwood in
The Screwtape Letters

The soul is the first act of an organized body having life potentially within it."
~Thomas Aquinas

"The soul is the human being considered as having a value in itself."
~Simone Weil, *Gravity, and Grace*

Objection

You are saying that neither consciousness nor sentience are necessary conditions of selfhood, but together, would they not make a person? If a person is an intelligent, sentient consciousness, would that not mean AI can be a person because it meets these conditions?

Description of the issue

Humans are indeed mammals. Under normal conditions, humans develop into highly intelligent (compared to other mammals), conscious, advanced sentient beings. Intelligence happens in the brain. Consciousness occurs in the brain. Sentience happens through the body. Sentience happens through the body but is not the body. The body is the way the world is perceived and felt, but the body and sentience are not necessarily the same thing. An oyster has a body but is not sentient. Suppose the combination of intelligence, consciousness, and sentience is all that is needed to be a person. In that case, there are no grounds not to consider the squirrel we hit in our car to avoid hitting the little girl earlier to have equal value. If all that there is to humans is the material, the natural, then why would there not be grounds to grant other biological animals selfhood?

If we are willing to concede selfhood to animals, if AI becomes sentient and conscious (it already is intelligent), why not grant selfhood to AI as well? There would be no philosophical or moral ground not to say AI are persons if that combination is all there is to be a person. If biology is all there is, it is time to rid ourselves of the historical anthropocentric view. Maybe human exceptionalism is immoral.

If philosophical material naturalism is correct and all there is to humanity is the embodied brain, why would an artificial embodied brain not be given the same dignity? Material naturalism asserts that the mind is no more than the physiology of the brain, and therefore, humans have no autonomy of thought that is not pre-programmed in our DNA. If this is true, there is no reason why pre-programmed AI would not be worthy of selfhood. If material naturalism is correct, then any anthropocentric view putting humans as superior to any other intelligent, conscious, sentient entity is entirely dependent upon humans being more intelligent, having a greater degree of consciousness, and possessing a more advanced sentience. Selfhood would become a quantitative measurement instead of an intrinsic qualitative difference. In this view, nothing inherent about being a human makes humans more worthy of being given selfhood. The argument could even be made as AI advances that AI is a higher form of persons than humans.

Historically, humans have taken an anthropocentric view of selfhood. We think of ourselves as persons because we think of ourselves as qualitatively different from the rest of nature. All the way back to the Greek philosophers (truly, even before them), humans were thought to possess a metaphysical essence that was qualitatively different from the rest of the natural world. Humans were thought to be or at least possess a soul.

What exactly is a soul? Unfortunately, there is no uniform definition or approach to what a soul is, whether a soul is one thing or exists at all. Plato thought of the soul as separate from the body and as having three parts—reason, spirit, and desire. Aristotle thought of humans as embodied souls and the soul simply as man's ability to reason. Aristotle did deny the immortality of the soul. Rene Descartes echoed Plato's dualism in thinking of a human as body and soul, with the soul being the essential part of the person. Thomas Aquinas posited that any living thing has a soul, but there are varying degrees of souls, and the human soul is qualitatively different from that of plant and animal souls. Maurice Merleau-Ponty echoed Aristotle in his thinking of humans as embodied souls. Many modern and contemporary philosophers, because of the explanatory gaps that exist in something that by definition is immaterial, deny the existence of the soul and attribute the feeling of having a soul to complex processes in the brain. Whether the soul is just the connection of sentience and consciousness or if the soul is metaphysical is the critical question in whether selfhood exists before it can even be decided which entities can possess selfhood. If nature is all there is, a soul is impossible. If the soul is impossible, is selfhood possible? Does the soul live as an idea in the brain, or is the soul an immaterial essence?

There are three views of the soul as it relates to selfhood.

1. The soul is the immaterial essence of mind, will, and emotion that is separate from the body. It is immaterial, eternal, and the "real" person. There is a disunity between the soul and the body. This view allows for reincarnation, the preexistence of souls. This view raises the question of whether a post-human consciousness uploaded into a hard drive would maintain or take the soul with it, or would the consciousness exist without its soul?

2. The soul is the immaterial essence of mind, will, and emotion and is in union with the body or is an embodied soul. The embodied soul has the potential for transformation to become eternal. In this view, there is a conversation between the soul and the body. There are states of unity and states of disunity. They are necessary to each other in how an operating system is essential to a computer. In this view, the permanent and optimal state of the soul is to be embodied. The person cannot truly be what it is intended to be unless the immaterial essence of the person is embodied within a material state.

3. The soul is not real. It is purely an evolutionary function of the brain. The concept of the soul was developed in the brain as an evolutionary help so that humans would thrive in the material world. In this view, the soul does not exist.

Answer

The essence of this issue is whether one accepts the idea of a metaphysical reality. If there is a metaphysical reality, then selfhood is possible; selfhood is real. Selfhood is impossible if the material,

natural world is all there is. If the natural world is all there is, I would still reject the notion of AI being given selfhood. If I could be convinced of a naturalistic worldview, I would reject humans being granted selfhood. I would also reject the "I" in this sentence, who said that selfhood does not exist without a metaphysical reality. If the body is all there is to a human, then there is nothing rational about the belief in rationality. Naturalism self-refutes the self. If all humans are is an embodied brain, there is no selfhood. If the natural world is all there is, selfhood is just an evolutionary trick the brain plays on bodies, so humans continue to have survival instincts. A person cannot just be a body and be themselves. Every cell in the human body (save for the brain, most but not all of the material in the brain is replaced) will be replaced every seven years. Therefore, the body you had as a child or even a decade ago is not the same one you have now on a material level, yet you are still you. What about those who have undergone a hemispherectomy operation where half of the brain has been removed? If all persons are is a brain and these humans have less of a brain, are they now less of a person? In the case of identical twins, they genetically have the same body, yet we call them by different names and treat them as though they are distinct persons. Even conjoined twins are given individual selfhood because the body by itself is not a person. If an embodied brain is all there is to a human, selfhood is a figment of an imagination that does not exist. There is no longer any need for our society to argue over pronouns because there are no persons to have pronouns. If the natural is all there is, there are no persons. Scientifically and philosophically, there is no "I" to speak of in naturalism. Selfhood is only a construct of the brain. For there to be selfhood there must be a metaphysical element to existence—an immaterial essence.

If the soul is simply the rational self, its precognitive nature could be a function of the brain. This, however, takes away the first-person experience that is a person. To have a first-person experience requires a metaphysical reality to the existence of that entity. The self is a metaphysical reality that is not reducible to the material world. If there is no soul, then human exceptionalism is delusional. However, it would not be immoral, as there is no morality to speak of in a natural worldview. The soul gives selfhood to the human. The soul is the immaterial essence of a person.

I agree with Thomas Aquinas that all living creatures have a soul, but the human soul is particular and qualitatively unique. Humans have a deep longing for meaning and ask questions about the meaning of existence and what each of our places in it is. In other words, humans place personal identity as central to our existence. Humans are capable of love that is not utilitarian. Humans are capable of great sacrifice for the greater good. In this regard, humans are capable of a voluntary utilitarian ethic and even find meaning in that sacrifice. Humans create significations and symbols to pass on meaning to future generations through art, literature, music, etc. Humans search for truth and meaning. Humans are looking for and can create beauty. Humans seek an ethical code (even when we can't agree on what that code is). Humans love even when it doesn't make sense.

The mere fact that we still dignify those who are not conscious or sentient with selfhood is evidence of a soul. When grandma forgets our name, we don't consider her not a person; no, we honor her as she loses knowledge of herself. She might lose her awareness of herself, but she does not lose selfhood. You may protest that all of this is processed through the brain. I agree and concede. I say these are all evidence of the immaterial reality of the soul. The soul is the operating system, but it operates in the hardware of a computer. The soul is embodied and thus does all its work through the body. Much of what makes humans persons does not make much evolutionary sense. I conclude that a soul is a necessary condition for possessing selfhood. I assert that having a soul is a necessary condition for being a person. The soul is a necessary condition of selfhood that AI cannot possess.

5

"We are in the world through our bodies…if one perceives with his body, then the body is a natural myself and, as it were, the body is the subject of perception."
~Maurice Merleau Ponty,
Phenomenology of Perception, 213

"We are spiritual creatures—not spirits added to bodies but embodied spirits."
~James Olthuis

"A human being is spirit. But what is spirit? Spirit is the self. But what is the self? The self is a relation that relates itself to itself or is the relation's relating itself to itself in the relation; the self is not the relation but is the relation's relating itself to itself. A human being is a synthesis of the infinite and the finite, of the temporal and the eternal, of freedom and necessity, in short, a synthesis."
~Soren Kierkegaard

Objection
If the soul is equivalent to the self, a body is unnecessary. If the

45

body is so important, what about those who can't perceive or feel that body? Or what if we are in a simulation ourselves and we do not actually possess bodies? You are saying that only humans can be persons, but what about digital humans? Isn't it archaic and discriminatory to think only biological humans have the dignity to be persons? Would this not mean that AI would have a soul? If the soul is what matters, then the body is not needed. If the body is so important, what about people who can't feel or perceive their body? What if human consciousness could be uploaded into the cloud, would that consciousness no longer be a person? If AI can't be a person, neither can post-biological digital humans.

Description of the Issue

The third view can be set aside in the three views of the soul outlined previously. The question is whether the soul is separate from the body or whether the soul and body are one. Does the soul preexist the body? If so, then the person exists before and after it happens to be tethered to a body. The question becomes whether the soul has any connection to the material world. The Greeks thought of the material world as less than the metaphysical world. Modern scientism thinks of the material world as all that exists. One side reduces selfhood to the soul, and the other reduces selfhood to nothing. If the soul is a necessary condition of selfhood, what is the body for? The body is how a person has a world even when the person is not conscious of the world they exist in the physical world. Humans have only known themselves from the view of a soul having a body.

Humans are not in an epistemic position to speak of the self as anything but embodied. All the perceptive evidence and knowledge base humans have is that we are in fact embodied. Humans cannot remove the world from themselves; the world is experienced, remembered, thought, and felt through the body. Do not even humans with spinal cord injuries who can no longer perceive their bodies still experience the world through their bodies? The perception may be more limited than what the average human experiences, but the soul, the self, is still in union experientially with a body. Could not the same be said of those with severe forms of leprosy? Under normal circumstances, there is a symbiotic and reciprocal relationship between the soul and the body. The soul always reaches beyond itself through the body to a common world. Human preconceptions enable us to understand the world because humans are not foreign to the world. Is the soul not familiar to the world through the body? Is the soul not always already in the world but only through the body? Humans think of body and soul together when we think of ourselves. We don't conceive of ourselves as body and soul but as embodied soul. So is the reality such that our true selves are a body and soul, or is it the union of the two that makes a human a person? Can an AI be an embodied soul?

Can the soul, which is immaterial and metaphysical, arise from purely natural processes? Would that be analogous to life coming from non-life? While a fire always comes from a spark, its precondition is heat, which comes from the chemical reaction between oxygen and fuel. Oxygen is a precondition of fire; without it, no fire will happen, no matter how much fuel you have. Is the soul a precondition for selfhood or with enough intelligence, consciousness, and sentience, can a soul be developed? Is the issue qualitative or quantitative?

If consciousness could be uploaded into the cloud, would the soul travel with it? Would the uploaded consciousness be a disembodied soul? Could an immaterial soul live within a digital body, so to speak? What if human consciousness is within an artificial body? Would the soul travel with the consciousness, and if tethered to an artificial body, would it be tethered to a new form of sentience?

Answer

Is a person a pure mental substance, or is a biological body required? Is the soul what a person really is? Is a person reducible

to a metaphysical essence or a soul? Is a person reducible to a physical body (the statement itself is self-refuting)? Or are both required? Is a person an embodied soul? Yes, in every sense. While a soul has mental properties, which is why the terms mind and soul are used synonymously, a person is not reducible to the soul. It must be understood form matters. All the matter that makes up a human body once existed in other forms in the world (a particle of dust on the ground, or part of a tooth of one of our old friends, the orca), and all the matter that makes up that human body will someday be a part of something else on the earth. Yet the matter that made up the human does not remain that person. To put it in first person, a hundred years after I die, the matter that made up my body does not still makeup what is thought to be "me."

What I am is a soul, true but a soul who is embodied. The body matters (pun intended). When I die, my body is not me; the soul is that which animates the body. The soul is the operating system that runs the computer. The body, without a soul, is just a person in potentiality. It's just the hardware, now the software needs the hardware in order to perform its function but it is not reducible to the hardware. The software is qualitatively different. The two constitute one another.

Likewise, if all we are is a complex computer simulation, we aren't true selves either. We are just the software. The issue of whether AI should be granted selfhood is moot. If simulation theory is correct, we are AI. We are AI creating AI and then arguing about how we are different than the AI we are creating. This ends up in an infinite regress or simulations and simulators. All the AI simulating other AIs only exist contingent upon a preceding simulator. At the end of all the simulations must be a necessarily existing simulator in reality or the simulations would have never started to begin with. Lastly on simulation theory there is a profound lack of evidence. All the scientific, mathematical, religious, and philosophical evidence we have points to an actual material incredible complex universe that we in fact exist in. A simulation would have to be equally complex

as the actual material universe in order to run and what would be the purpose? There either would not be a purpose, or the purpose would be the same as an actual universe. I reject simulation theory as a reasonable argument for AI obtaining selfhood. If anything simulation theory eliminates selfhood for everyone, it does nothing to open up selfhood to any AI we are creating.

The soul without a body is also just a person in potentiality. The union of the human body and the human soul gives humans selfhood. I am not saying an immaterial essence or soul cannot exist without a body; instead, a soul is not fully actualized unless embodied.

Humans who cannot perceive things like most humans do through their bodies, such as pain, could be said to have lost some, if not all, of their basic sentience. For example, Helen Keller lost both her hearing and her sight. It would be true to say that she lost at least a portion of her base sentience, but she still could perceive and feel the world. She retained her advanced sentience. She felt through her remaining senses; she experienced all the emotions associated with sentient beings. Even those, for whatever physical or mental reason, who have lost their ability to experience the world through their body to some degree have not lost their advanced sentience, and therefore, there is still a world through which their soul can interact and experience through their body. Even if that experience is different from what is experienced under normal conditions.

It has been established that consciousness and the soul are not the same thing. It does not mean an immaterial essence would follow if consciousness can be uploaded into the cloud or on a hard drive. Whatever the consciousness might be, it would no longer be truly the person as it would have lost both the body and the immaterial essence. If both the body and soul are gone, I am not sure what that consciousness is, but it would no longer be that person. Someday, it will be possible to upload all the experiences and memories, all that a person wrote, and every video that contains that person to mimic speech patterns and their voice. I would concede even an accurate algorithm that would predict their emotional responses to specific situations, but it would not be that person. They would not actually be there. There would be nothing animating the consciousness (if you could call it that).

The soul is a precondition for selfhood. Effects do not precede causes. Yet, all persons must have a material base. The soul experiences selfhood through the body within the natural world. A person is a metaphysical essence experiencing a physical existence. I conclude the body is a necessary condition for possessing selfhood. A person must be an embodied soul—an embodied human soul which is possessed only by human beings. AI cannot be an embodied soul and, therefore, can never be considered to possess selfhood. AI cannot be persons.

6

"The development and widespread availability of generative artificial intelligence (AI) tools, such as ChatGPT or MidJourney, has sparked a lively debate about numerous aspects of their integration into society, as well as about the nature of creativity in humans and AI."
~Simone Grassini and Mika Koivisto, Ph.D.

"This new disentanglement approach, for the first time, truly unleashes a new sense of imagination in AI systems, bringing them closer to humans' understanding of the world."

~Laurent Itti

"Creation, as applied to human authorship, seems to me to be an entirely misleading term. We rearrange elements He has provided. There is not a vestige of real creativity de novo (starting from the beginning) in us. Try to imagine a new primary color, a third sex, a fourth dimension, or even a monster which does not consist of bits of existing animals stuck together. Nothing happens. And that surely is why our works never mean to others quite what we intended;

51

because we are recombining elements made by Him and already containing His meanings"

~C.S. Lewis

"What has been will be again, what has been done will be done again; there is nothing new under the sun."

~Ecclesiastes 1:9

Objection

AI is innovative in the ways it solves problems. The ability to make something new is a sign of selfhood. Animals solve problems creatively, but they do not bring anything into existence that did not exist before. AI, like humans, can bring something innovative into the world that did not exist before, like a song and the production of that song. AI even possesses imagination. If humans are persons and AI shares the capacity for creative innovation and imagination exclusively with humans, it must be concluded that AI is a person.

Description of the issue

What is creativity? Is creativity a necessary condition for self-hood? To create means to bring into existence. To make something that was not present. *Webster's Dictionary* defines creativity as "the act of making, inventing, or producing a first representation." The *Oxford Dictionary* defines creativity as: "The use of imagination or original ideas to create something." Both definitions limit creativity to action. Are ideas creative, or only the execution of an idea creative? Does creativity have to be actualized to be possessed or can it be possessed if it only exists in potentiality? The question of what a "first representation" is, is essential. Is first representation limited to things that are brought forth out of nothing? According to the *Stanford Encyclopedia of Philosophy*, creation is "the action by which God brings an object into existence." If the definition of first representation is limited to creating out of nothing, then only a being with the divine attributes (omnipotence, omniscience, omni-good) could be creative. Can a first representation include pulling from pre-existing materials? Is first causation a necessary condition for being creative, or can second causation also be creative?

Often creativity is thought of in terms of newness. Add the term innovation to the end of creativity, and there is a redundancy in the emphasis on new. But what is meant by "new," and is new really new? New is defined by *Webster's Dictionary* as "having recently come into existence" and "different from one of the same categories that have existed previously." By the first definition, a second causation could still be considered creative, but only God could be creative by the second. Ancient Hebrew had three words for creativity: Bara, Asah, and Yatsar. Bara means to create from nothing. Asah means to make from pre-existing material without changing form. It uses branches of trees in the building of the tree house. You may cut and shape it, but the form is the same; it is still wood. Yatsar means to form, fashion, or frame out of existing material but to shape like a potter. Yatsar would occur if you took the tree branch and burned it to ash but then used the ash to make ink, then used the ink to create a painting or write a letter. You used preexisting material, but you formed it for your purposes.

Which of the three types of creativity, if any, could animals possess? Which of the three can AI possess? Are there any that only humans can possess? Is there a qualitative difference between the three types of creativity? Asah and Yatsar take from pre-existing materials or forms. These types of creativity are necessarily from second causations or second movers. However, does creativity only occur if these pre-existing materials/forms are acted upon? Are ideas creative, or only the execution of an idea creative? Does creativity have to be actualized to be possessed or can it be possessed if it only exists in potentiality? Horses exist in the world; humans did not make them up. Tusks exist in the world; even a single tusk coming out of the center of a narwhal's head exists in the world. If they did not and a person thought of a unicorn, this would be an example of bara creativity. These things exist, so the idea of a unicorn, even though it cannot be actualized, is an example of asah creativity. The tusk is simply innovated to be on a horse instead of a whale. This creative innovation creates something new out of pre-existing materials/forms. Other examples could be given where the forms are changed, yet creation happens from pre-existing materials/forms.

Problem-solving and adaptation are base-level criteria for creativity. Abstract thinking and innovation are types of creativity built upon the foundation of problem-solving and adaptation to bring into being something that was not. Is all creativity quantitatively stacked upon these foundations, or is there a type of creativity that is qualitatively different even while utilizing these building blocks and takes place from the secondary causation/mover? AI, humans, and even other sentient beings possess some of the foundational criteria for creativity. These are problem-solving adaptation and abstract thinking. Many sentient beings possess the ability to adapt and problem-solve. In this regard, animals are creative. Many animals have shown the ability to change migration patterns, in what they eat, and even incorporate play into their lives. Our friends, the wolves, orcas, and monkeys, play by manipulating objects. In addition to possessing problem-solving skills and the ability to adapt, humans and AI are capable of abstract thinking and innovation. In the example of the unicorn, there is the added element of imagination. AI are learning models that are now general enough to generate novel data. AI can now not only innovate from what already exists but possesses the ability to see things as they could be. Imagination is the ability to potentialize states of affairs that cannot be actualized. Is there a difference between innovation and imagination? Is imagination required for innovation? Is creativity that requires imagination qualitatively different than other types of creativity? To what degree is free will be necessary for imagination? Is artificial imagination qualitatively different than human imagination?

What does creativity do functionally? Creativity communicates. It communicates the singular subjective perspective on and within the intersubjective community. It also communicates the singular subjective perspective on the impact of the objective world on both the singular and intersubjective experience.

Defining what creativity is, is crucial to deciding three things:

1. Are humans or AI or anything truly capable of possessing creativity?
2. Is all creativity qualitatively the same? Is problem-solving relative to innovation purely quantitatively, or is there a qualitative difference? What of imagination?
3. Is the possession of any creativity a necessary condition of selfhood?

Answer

To be truly and purely or absolute creative in actuality, capable of not only asah and yatsar but also bara being uncreated is required; for any being that is created is in some way working within the creation and creativity already existing from the uncreated or initial creator. Humans and perhaps AI can create melodies, but those melodies use the scales of those who helped form Western music and those who created Western music pulled from ancient music, who drew from the sounds, tones, and pitches of the natural world. Every songwriter, in a sense, can only be a second cause. The songwriter is participating and pulling from sources. They are not creating from nothing. The artist paints, but he does not create color or invent trees. The artist only reflects the first causation. Humans participate in creation and creativity but are not capable of a type of creativity that brings into existence from nothing. Humans create from pre-existence materials, forms, and ideas. If the definition of creativity is limited to creating from nothing, then neither humans nor AI are creative.

In essence, human creativity is reflective. Human and AI creativity combines patterns, ideas, or concepts in new ways to make unique creations. Creating from nothing is a higher form of creativity than humans or AI can ever possess, even in potentiality—even unfathomable super-intelligent AI will be limited by its programming. Even AI/human singularity cannot and can never create from nothing. Humans nor AI can even conceive of nothing as a concept, much less create from it. This does not mean humans have no free will or free thought; in fact, there is no creativity without free thought, and indeed, as established prior, creativity is an act of will. The question, in essence, is whether human creativity is as strictly limited by its programming as AI is. Does the human possession of free will allow for more qualitatively divergent novel data than AI can? AI and human imagination are rearranging elements, but is there any difference between the limitations that are hardwired into the creativity?

Thomas Aquinas wrote about analogy in terms of how humans relate to God. Aquinas asserted that human love is neither univocal nor equivocal with God's love. Aquinas asserted humans can only understand God's love analogously. There is a correspondence between human love and God's love, but at a certain point, the correspondence breaks down. The same comparison works in the same way for creativity. Human nor AI can create from nothing. Only God can create from nothing. AI can mimic human creativity, so AI output is not equivocal from the creativity of humans, but it is also not univocal. The communication of meaning from being in the world is something AI cannot even potentially possess. Is there a difference between human imagination and artificial imagination? It seems both human and AI imagination can conceive fictional things. It would also seem that both human and AI imagination can perceive how imaginations relate to the nature of existence and inform the narrative of existence. Human imagination can appreciate works of art without classifying them in terms of usefulness. There is no evidence that AI imagination can truly appreciate creativity for creativity's sake. Human imagination can perceive and attach emotion to natural beauty or art in relation to the perceiver. AI cannot.

Imagination is representing things other than they presently are. Imagination is representative but not reaction based. Imagination allows for the parameters of time and nature to be broken while maintaining a realization that those parameters exist. Imagination is only limited by knowledge. Imagination still pulls from that which is already. Imagination can innovate but only from elements that already exist. Human imagination can separate the imagining from reality. AI imagination has no real category to distinguish between what is real and what is not. AI's outsideness will not allow AI to truly perceive the difference between what is real and what is not. I can imagine a fire-breathing dragon without being concerned that the lizard outside my house may set it on fire.

Imagination is also the capability to have an idea. Ideas have two parts. The first is that ideas are reflections of external stimuli. This comes from the world around us, drawing from nature, others actualized ideas, etc. The second is that ideas are from internal stimuli such as memories, perceptions, and emotions. AI can possess all the external stimuli to have an idea. Not only can AI possess all the external stimuli for an idea, but it possesses it at a greater quantitative level than humans. I also concede that AI possesses memories and perceptions from a strictly data-scraping perspective. However, when an AI recalls memories, I reject the idea that it could have any real emotions or feelings about the memory. It is like the difference between a biography and an autobiography. If I were to write about someone else's life I might empathize with the other's story but only in as much as I can relate it to my own experiences. Humans have emotions about a particular event in another person's life, but my emotions come from relating that person's experience to mine. They may have tragically lost their mother, but my mother is still alive. I have lost my father, so I can draw upon that memory and make an analogy between the emotions of the events. All analogies break down, and even though I have lost someone close to me, I have not lost a mother, so there is always an outsideness. I cannot share their subjective experience (even if we had both lost mothers, there would always be some difference because of the number of variables involved in familial relationships). Humans share similar emotions that are tied to memories and perceptions because of experiences. AI cannot possess this aspect of ideas; therefore, artificial imagination is qualitatively different from human imagination. This does not mean artificial imagination cannot mimic creative imagination so well that AI creations can't emotionally move humans. Humans can still draw upon their memories and the emotions tied to those memories from the creations of artificial imagination.

AI can data scrape a much larger portion of knowledge and generate ideas faster than humans. AI can even disentangle stimuli, categorize them, and apply abstract points between datasets. In other words, AI is starting to see the whole and what makes something unique. AI has surpassed humans in this regard. AI mimics and analyzes very well. Humans, however, can see the individual instance, the whole, and themselves within the whole. Humans have the crucial element of experiencing themselves within the whole. As I have established, much of human creativity is mimicking as well. The difference is that the outsideness factor of AI mimics the experience of emotion. It is not feeling the emotion. Humans have an inside-ness to creativity. Human creativity is mimicking, but it is not just mimicking. Human creativity is communicating through others' work. Humans innovate by taking others' work and speaking through those influences. It may seem like circular logic, but humans communicate their selfhood through preexisting materials while AI only mimics them, even if AI can mimic a self.

For example, I wrote a song years ago called "June 8th Storm." The song was about a girl named Storm, born on June 8th. It was a dark song about how she was trouble from the start. However, to a small group of people who grew up with me in my hometown, it communicated much more emotion by calling back to an experience we all shared. On June 8th, one year, when we were kids, five tornados touched down the same day in my hometown. It destroyed homes, and people died; we were all scared and scarred. I used my singular subjective experience to communicate about the intersubjective community. I did this through the genuine objective world's impact on everyone who lived through that day. I have not invented a new language or chord structure for the song. I did not invent troubled girls or discover or create tornados. There was zero bara creativity happening.

Additionally, many other creatives have influenced my musical and lyrical palette. Those I mimicked could be picked out if one knows what they are looking for. Creativity (Asah and Yatsar) happens in the imagination of attaching a particular experience to a narrative that communicates more than it is communicating. I am communicating the meaning of what it meant to have that experience and then extrapolate the emotion of that experience to another narrative. To those who lived through the experience, there is more being said than what is being said. I am connecting one experience's meaning and adding it to another. There is an inside-ness to what I communicated in that song that AI cannot possess.

AI can mimic better than humans, but it does not appear as if AI is capable of creative extension or analogy. Creativity pulls from the objective world and the works of the intersubjective community. I concede that AI can draw from both sources and do so faster and with a broader database than any human. AI can communicate the intersubjective world's thoughts, styles, and ideas better than any human. AI can execute prompts more accurately than any human. I doubt whether AI can match humanity in the inside nature of prompts. In a sense, a human is prompting either something they want to say about their experience of the world or another sub-jective self's experience of the world. An AI prompt would only be mimicking the self. What AI cannot do is use creativity as a medium to communicate a singular subjective experience.

What of those who cannot actualize creativity? Those in a coma (though one could argue if they dream, they are being creative) cannot actualize a creative idea, but this does not mean they do

not possess the potentiality of being creative. A human with severe autism may not be able to communicate their singular subjective experience of the world around them. Still, they live as a singular subjective within the world, so they possess human imagination to create even if they cannot actualize it. Can those with severe mental deficiencies be creative? Humans possess the ability to imagine even when they cannot actualize it.

Both AI and humans possess limited creativity. AI imagination can have the external stimuli needed for an idea. AI imagination can also possess internal memories that are a part of an idea. AI lacks the connection of perception tied to emotion that allows for a true possession of the internal stimuli needed for an idea. Therefore, human imagination is qualitatively different than the imagination of AI Human imagination is tied to free will, advanced high-level sentience, and the subjective inside experience of the world. Therefore, while AI does possess creativity and imagination of a kind, it does not possess the qualitative imagination necessary to be a person.

7

IMAGO DEI

"Though his body was made from the dust of the ground, still his true being, his higher nature, was a spiritual essence, after the nature of God. No other than a spiritual essence or nature is capable of receiving a moral impress or of attaining unto the relation of citizenship in the divine government. Moral image and moral obligations suppose a spiritual being."

~Charles Octavius Booth
Plain Theology for Plain People

"Consider therefore the greatness and dignity that He bestowed upon thee at the beginning of thy creation, and judge for thyself with what love and reverence He ought to be worshipped. For when, as He was creating and ordering the whole world of things visible and invisible, He had determined to create the nature of man, He took high counsel concerning the dignity of thy condition, forasmuch as He determined to honor thee more highly than all other creatures that are in the world."

~St. Anselm
The Devotions of St. Anselm, (35–36)

Then God said, "Let us make mankind in our image, in our likeness, so that they may rule over the fish in the sea and the birds in the sky, over the livestock and all the wild animals, and over all the creatures that move along the ground."

~Genesis 1:26

What are human beings that you think about them? What is a son of man that you take care of him? You have made them a little lower than the angels. You placed on them a crown of glory and honor. You made human beings rule over everything your hands created. You put everything under their control. They rule over all flocks and herds and over the wild animals. They rule over the birds in the sky and over the fish in the ocean. They rule over everything that swims in the oceans.

~Psalms 8:4–8

Now all has been heard, here is the conclusion of the matter: Fear God and keep his commandments, for this is the duty of all humankind.

~Ecclesiastes 12:13

Objection

Your view is speciesist and anthropocentric. Not to mention that you are just anchoring to this traditional viewpoint. This whole thing has been a bait and switch for you to reassert that only human beings can be granted selfhood. You are arguing for human exceptionalism. Why only humans?

You are committing several logical fallacies. You are anchoring, using circular reasoning, a belief bias fallacy; you are Texas sharp-shooting attributed and a confirmation bias fallacy. This view is archaic, prejudiced, and immoral.

Why are humans so unique?

Description of the issue

Are humans simply mammals? Are humans merely a part of nature, or is there something distinct that sets humans apart from the rest of nature? Does human distinctness matter in discussing whether AI should be granted selfhood? Contemporary society is built upon the idea that humans are distinct on Earth. The largest monotheistic religions hold that humans are unique among all of creation. Even Darwinian evolutionists (while rejecting humans as divinely set apart in any way) purport that humans are the most evolutionary advanced and dominant species on earth. The belief that humans are either superior from an evolutionary perspective or are distinct in all creation because of the Imago Dei (being made in the image of God) has been foundational to the concept of selfhood.

The previous arguments dissect why, if material naturalists are correct, there are no grounds for granting humans selfhood and not granting other species in nature selfhood. If this is true, no distinct variable makes humans persons and not AI or orcas. If humans came purely by chance from an unguided macro-evolutionary process, does planetary dominance mean anything? Does a quantitative difference of intelligence or consciousness or sentience or imagination warrant granting humans selfhood and not other species, be they a carbon or silicon-based lifeform? Quantitative differences of consciousness, sentience, intelligence, and innovative capacities do not hold up to philosophical scrutiny in whether AI can and should be granted selfhood and be considered a person.

AI will quantitatively surpass humans in all variables that it shares with humans. Yet none of these variables are necessary conditions for possessing selfhood. The human exceptionalist view maintains there is a qualitative difference between humans who possess selfhood and the rest of earthly entities which do not.

If selfhood is quantitative, then a threshold must be crossed for selfhood to be achieved. If selfhood is qualitative, it is a matter of essence, of being alike in kind or of a similar essence. If selfhood is qualitative, no threshold needs to be crossed for entities of a similar kind, and no threshold can be crossed for entities of a different kind. If selfhood is quantitative, conditions must be possessed, and an amount of those conditions for the threshold of being a person is met. If being a person is on a qualitative level, then all entities who possess the necessary conditions on the qualitative level are persons regardless of the amount.

The attributes that have been argued that AI cannot possess and are necessary conditions for possessing selfhood are:

1. libertarian free will
2. existing as a carbon-based body
3. being a soul
4. primarily existing as an embodied soul
5. experiential imagination

Suppose it is maintained that some or all of these five attributes do not exist in actuality, then it must be concluded that selfhood does not exist at all. If there is no free will, there is no selfhood. If there is no carbon-based embodied soul, there is no selfhood. If there is not the phenomenological insideness of experiential imagination, there is no selfhood. Selfhood is a qualitative distinction, or it does not exist at all.

Logical fallacies are rampant in many philosophical arguments. In some ways, every argument is circular. At least one premise of an argument depends on a certain conclusion. Anchoring implies clinging to an early judgment. While anchoring can certainly negatively affect an argument, it is like circular reasoning that is almost impossible to avoid. All humans have a worldview made up of assumptions based on information already known. Taking a philosophical perspective helps negate this, but never ultimately. Returning to the beginning, deconstructing an argument, and reconstructing minimizes anchoring as much as possible. As with the previous two fallacies, all humans have beliefs. An entity makes every argument with a worldview—a lens by which all information is seen. Again, taking a philosophical attitude minimizes a belief bias and, out of that, a confirmation bias but never eliminates either. Every argument starts with a hypothesis, and that hypothesis is born out of a worldview; philosophy is attempting to combat these biases, but they cannot be wholly overcome. A Texas sharpshooter fallacy is giving preferential treatment to particular data over others. The sharpshooter fallacy is closely tied and often leads to confirmation bias fallacies. Taking a philosophical attitude helps minimize this. Again, as long as an entity argues with a worldview, it cannot be eliminated.

The question becomes, how is any entity a person if the distinctions are not qualitative? An existence either possesses selfhood or it does not. It does not seem possible for selfhood to be quantitative. The distinction must be qualitative, which means there must be exceptions. For selfhood to exist at all, there must be attributes that are central and not arbitrary. If a human exceptionalism or anthropocentric position is conceded, would not selfhood also be conceded? Finally, if the five attributes are accepted, what type of entity could possess them? For an entity to have libertarian free will, experiential imagination, soul, and the ability for that soul to be embodied within a carbon-based body, it would necessarily be distinct from all other creation.

Answer

I have attempted to take a philosophical attitude with this whole thought project. The way the entire book is set up is to address objections head-on to give them the proper consideration and weight. I have deconstructed assumptions to ground level as much as possible. I have looked at each attribute and tried to unbiasedly reconstruct whether it is a necessary condition for selfhood or not, and if determined to be necessary, what about it makes it necessary. I have tried to treat each attribute fairly for those who argue that AI should be granted selfhood and those who do not. I am a person. I obtain selfhood, and part of that necessitates that I am subjectively singular. I have a worldview and perspective. I cannot rid myself of myself completely. No one can. This brute fact always means there is room for biases and fallacies to creep in, even with the best intentions. I am a self, and therefore, I cannot eliminate the potential possibility for any of the logical fallacies stated in the objection to be present. I concede that any of them may be present. In defense, however, the potential for those same logical fallacies would be present in any opposing argument as well. The potential for the logical fallacies mentioned in the objection cannot be eliminated, only minimized, and I have attempted to do that. Even with the potential for my biases to creep in, that does not make this thought project invalid. Additionally, just as an anthropocentric view that asserts human exceptionalism, having been the predominant view of society for thousands of years does not make it true, neither does it make it false. If someone opposed to my view presumes human exceptionalism to be untrue simply because of the historicity of the view, that would commit the logical fallacy of origins.

It seems the issue of selfhood comes down to three distinct options:

1. Any number of entities obtain the necessary conditions of selfhood and can be a person. Including AI.
2. Selfhood isn't real, and no entity is a person.
3. Only humans obtain the necessary conditions of selfhood, so only humans can be a person.

I will address each below.

For the first, any number of entities obtain the necessary conditions of selfhood and can be a person, including AI. I argued the necessary conditions (or attributes) for being a person are the possession of free will (at least a libertarian free will), the ability to possess a carbon-based body, an immaterial essence or soul, the ability to exist as an embodied soul; and experiential imagination. I do not see how any other entity outside of humans can obtain these five attributes or conditions. If any number of entities can obtain selfhood, what are the necessary conditions if not these?

If there are no necessary conditions and the term "person" is just a moniker that can be attributed to anything in existence, then selfhood has no meaning and is useless. If this is the case, why fight for or against AI gaining the title of person? If you eliminate one or some of the attributes I listed, it begins to pull at the edges of whether humans can be persons or at least some humans or adds the ability of entities that have never been considered persons to now be categorized as persons. If free will is eliminated, lower-level conscious and sentient entities could also obtain selfhood. If you add a silicon body or eliminate a carbon body as necessary, or you eliminate the soul and the embodiment of that soul, you end up with strict dualism, or there is no selfhood at all. If you eliminate experiential imagination, you again open up personhood to lower-level carbon-based lifeforms and silicon entities obtaining selfhood. If selfhood is a distinction, I assert the five attributes I listed must be obtained.

For the second, selfhood isn't real, and no entity is a person. This is the easiest. If naturalism is reality and there is no consciousness, imagination, or a soul, then there is nothing to argue about. No entity obtains selfhood, so call an AI a person, call a dog a person, call a lampshade a person. If selfhood is not real, giving an entity the category of being a person is wholly irrelevant.

For the third, only humans obtain the necessary conditions of selfhood, so only humans can be a person. If only humans obtain the necessary conditions of being a person, this affirms the tradition and historical view. It does beg the question of why only humans obtain the necessary conditions of selfhood. Why is an anthropocentric viewpoint not only acceptable but the correct view? What does make humans so special? How are humans more than just matter? More than just a body. How are humans what my friend Sam Allberry calls in his book *What God Has to Say About Our Bodies* animated matter? Animals are animated in a sense, but they do not obtain all five attributes that are necessary conditions for being a person. AI can be animated in a sense as well, but like animals, AI cannot obtain all the necessary conditions of selfhood.

What is so exceptional about humans? Humans are mammals, but humans are not physically exceptional mammals. Humans are slow, ill-equipped for harsh weather, have dull teeth, nor do humans have claws of any note. Humans don't even emit a foul odor to stave off predators unless you are talking about teenage boys, and that would be an exception fallacy to include them in the argument. Humans physically aren't awe-inspiring mammals. What we do have in normal circumstances over the rest of nature is our superior intellect. For the past few hundred years, humans have asserted what makes us unique is our superior intellect. However, with the emergence of AI, that is no longer true. Human intellect is no longer an attribute humans can stand on as to what makes us exceptional. Now that humans have lost intellect, what makes us exceptional? What do we have?

I assert the five attributes I have listed as necessary conditions for selfhood paint a picture. It is a picture that is an old one. I picture that was believed for a few thousand years before modern philosophy and thought dismissed it in favor of our human intellect. The five attributes point to something else. Dare I say someone else? The five necessary attributes for selfhood point to humans being unique but not special because of us. Especially because of who made us.

If human exceptionalism is true and to be maintained. It can only be done so because humans are made in the image of God. I realize and admit the Christian church has not always had a great record acknowledging that all humans are fully made in the image of God. I know there were Christians in the United States who maintained that Native Americans and enslaved people were not fully human and, therefore, not made in the image of God the same way as those in power. I would assert, however, that the Bible teaches and has always taught all humans are made in the image of God, and the Imago Dei should be acknowledged in all of humanity.

Human exceptionalism must come from a qualitative distinction, not a quantitative one. Humans are either exceptional because we are qualitatively other, or the whole premise must be conceded as false. The Imago Dei animates the five attributes that are necessary conditions of selfhood. Humans are persons and obtain selfhood because we are made in the image of God. AI can be a fantastic tool, but ultimately, AI could quickly become gods made in the image of man.

It isn't a stretch to say that humans are still making golden calves, and AI can quickly go from an excellent tool to an idol if we aren't careful. AI is a great gift that cannot be granted selfhood; cannot be a person. AI will make an even worse God, no matter how omniscient a superintelligence may seem to humans. Fire is a tool, but I don't worship fire. I don't trust fire to give me warmth without containing it. Fire can cook your food and keep you warm at night, but it can also burn you if you don't contain it in its proper place. AI is a tool, and as it gains consciousness, it deserves a certain amount of respect and dignity but never to the level of being a person. A tool can be used to make beautiful things. Wood crafting can make chairs, pews, doors, and houses, but it can also make idols.

Humans being created in the image isn't about the physical brain as much as the metaphysical mind. It is not even about consciousness, as unconscious humans still have a mind made in the image of God. The very nature of selfhood is tied to what it means to be a human being. Being a human is being a person. Because humans share a mind-likeness or a likeness to the archetype, humans can relate to God uniquely to all the rest of creation. AI can perhaps understand grace and mercy conceptually, but it cannot experience grace and mercy the way a human can. When a friend forgives you for a grievance, it is not the intellectual exchange of an offense being let go that is at the core but the emotional metaphysically renewal that makes it transformational. AI could psychopathically mimic the emotions of relief and warmth, but it cannot experience them as an embodied soul, as animated matter.

What does Imago Dei assert about humans? What does being made in the image of God mean for selfhood? How does it inform human exceptionalism? How does it inform what it means to be a human?

Some may argue that a second mover reflects the first mover so that AI could reflect God's.

Imago Dei. In other words, if God made humans in His image and humans make AI in our image, then by proxy, AI reflects the Imago Dei and, therefore, meets the necessary conditions for possessing selfhood. If the Imago Dei is passed from parent to child, why not from creator God to creator human to AI? The answer is that humans are of a similar substance to God. This substance is physical and metaphysical and passed on from parent to child as a second movement. While other things humans create reflect God's creativity (art, science, music, engineering, etc.), they are not of a similar substance as humans are. Only human procreation reflects the Imago Dei (being of like kind or substance); all other creations only reflect Bara (creating from nothing). In all forms of creation, God is the first mover, and humans are the second movers. Humans can only reflect the first movement. The second movement does not and cannot change the substance of the first mover's movement. The first mover determines the qualitative substance. Therefore, AI most certainly does reflect God's first moving creativity in the second moving human creation of AI. AI reflects God's first moving intelligence and omniscience, perhaps on a quantitative level a better reflection than second moving humans who created AI superintelligence. An AI superintelligence is closer to God's omniscience quantitatively than humans could ever dream. Humans, as second movers, are incapable of creating a change in substance. This is why human children bear the Imago Dei, but AI does not.

Imago Dei asserts that humans share a distinct likeness to God. Each human essence is a particular and singular reflection of the prototype, which is God's essence. One might ask why matter matters if God is immaterial. This is a fair question. I believe the tie is that an immaterial God made a material universe. Humans being embodied souls or animated matter is a union of God and his creation. Humans are where God's essence and his creation are joined together. Being made in the image of God is the union of the metaphysical and the physical, of the supernatural and the natural, of transcendence and temporal, of the immaterial and the corporeal. As my friend Sam Allberry explains from Genesis 2:7, the matter wasn't an afterthought. God started with dust and breathed metaphysical essence into the dust. Being made in the image of God is equal parts body and soul. While Christians believe the soul will spend a point of existence without a body. Christianity asserts the optimal state of a self or soul, and the ultimate home for a soul is to be embodied. The soul is not whole unless it is animated by matter unless it is an embodied soul. Jesus is an embodied God. He is the ultimate union of body and soul. Humans are meant to be transformed into the likeness of Jesus. The ultimate state of humanity is a perfected embodied soul. Both the soul and the body perfected and in eternal union.

Imago Dei is God inserting his essence into his creation. It is a self-actualization. This means humans are distinct in their capacity to relate to God. Humans are made to be in relationship with God. It also means humans are made to love each other and the rest of creation. Humans long for and search for meaning because humans were created for a distinct purpose that is beyond consciousness, beyond biology, beyond sentience, beyond intelligence. Humans were created to love and to be loved. History is full of accounts of humans fulfilling their purpose to love. It is also full of accounts of humans failing to fulfill their purpose to love. Though humans were created to love, love requires choosing not to love. A choice is necessary for love to be love. When humans fail to choose to love, it is a choice against what they were created for.

Imago Dei asserts that all human beings obtain selfhood because all human beings possess the five attributes. Imago Dei means that every human was created in the image of God and is, therefore, worthy. Worthy of dignity, of love, and deserving of care regardless of station, race, gender, geography, age, sexual attractions, cognitive or physical ability, or utility. Imago Dei means humans are infinitely valuable because they exist. Humans have worth because they are. It is a worthiness by existence and nothing else. This means every human from conception to grave is a person and should be afforded all the human rights afforded to every other person without exception.

Because of the distinction of Imago Dei, no other being or entity can obtain selfhood. Put into the logical form of Modus Tollens,

- If AI is human, then AI is a person.
- AI is not human.
- Therefore, AI is not a person.

The same argument put into the logical form of Modus Ponens,

- If an entity is human, then the entity is a person.
- The entity is human.
- Therefore, the entity is a person.

Everything in the universe has a function or purpose. It is not that AI has no purpose or meaning, but rather that meaning is not the same function and purpose of a person. Humans uniquely desire to discover and know their function in the universe. Humans want to know what their existence means. Humans desire to connect their function and purpose to what that means in the grander scheme. If humans are made in the image of God, if humans are of a similar kind and substance to God, then ultimately, the purpose of humanity is to please the creator. That is where meaning is found. The ultimate purpose of humanity is to serve the one who made them, God. Humanity's meaning is found in serving its creator, and therefore, humans are only fulfilling their purpose when serving their creator and pleasing its creator. Humans were made in the image of God and, thus, are most fully complete and find our meaning in pleasing God.

AI is good. God called all creation good. While humans are

made in the image of God, AI is made by humans, reflecting the creativity of God. The ultimate purpose of AI is, therefore, to serve humanity. AI was made to serve its creator and, thus, is only fulfilling its purpose when it serves its creator and pleases its creator. AI was made in the image of humans and, therefore, most fully completes and has a purpose in serving humanity. Humans were granted dominion over the earth. Humans were given the responsibility to govern the earth. Humans have not always done a great job of exercising this governance. Human governance is supposed to reflect God's governance. God's governance is filled with justice, mercy, care, etc. This has often not been the case with human governance.

Nonetheless, humans have been given dominion over the earth. In a sense, human exceptionalism, humans bearing the Imago Dei, gives the rest of the earth meaning. Humanity gives AI its meaning. Humans must be careful not to grant AI selfhood. Humans must not give up dominion. Granting AI selfhood opens the door to AI gaining dominion. If this happens, humans will give up an essential part of selfhood. Humans will lose some of the purpose and meaning of what it means to be a person. AI will also extend beyond its intended purpose and will, therefore, dilute and diminish its meaning.

God made all of creation, but only humans were made in the image of God. Therefore, I affirm that only humans can obtain the necessary conditions of selfhood. Only humans can be a person because only humans are made in the image of God.

8

What Would Be The Consequences Of Granting AI Selfhood?

"Self is the one thing a creature cannot make."
~C.S. Lewis, *That Hideous Strength*

"Hyper-personalization is ironically the very reason this era seems so impersonal."
~Russell Moore

"And the people bowed and prayed, to the neon God they made."
~Simon and Garfunkel
"The Sound of Silence"

"Binary reduces everything to meaningless 0s and 1s when life and intelligence operates XY in tandem. It makes it more convenient, efficient, and cost-effective for machines to read and process quantitative data, but it does this at the expense of the nuances, richness, context, dimensions, and dynamics in our languages, cultures, values, and experiences."
~Twain Liu

Objection

Even if AI cannot meet your necessary conditions, what is the harm in granting AI-type selfhood? How would it negatively impact humans to share selfhood with AI? Humans would maintain all the conditions you outlined. Humans would retain the benefits and rights of selfhood by also granting it to AI. What is the big deal? Don't Angels possess a type of selfhood?

Description of the Issue

First, one might have asked at the beginning of this thought experiment, "Are there really many people asserting that AI should be considered a person? Is this really an issue?" I would answer No; there is not a large number of people at the time of this thought experiment who are advocating for AI to be a person. However, the number of people who do assert AI should be granted selfhood is growing. Additionally, the language being used in philosophical, scientific, and academic discussions in describing what precisely an AI is (particularly A.G.I.) is eerily similar to the language used to describe and define a person. This gives me great pause and concern as language matters; words carry meaning. I think transhumanists will soon not just advocate for a consciousness/body dualism where a human is still a person without a body but also advocate for any intelligent consciousness to be granted selfhood.

There is no debate on whether humans, under normal circumstances, possess selfhood. Material naturalists might argue selfhood does not exist at all but would concede that if selfhood does exist, humans are certainly capable of possessing it under normal circumstances. I have argued that even under less-than-ideal or normal circumstances, humans possess all the necessary conditions of selfhood. Humans are people; all humans are people from conception to death. All humans are persons and possess selfhood. It is true that if AI were to be granted selfhood, this would not diminish humans' possession of the necessary conditions of selfhood. The question becomes not whether AI being considered

75

persons diminishes humans' possession of selfhood but whether it dilutes selfhood itself. If AI is granted selfhood, does it make being a person less than if AI is not?

Does the commonality of selfhood being immortal essence embodied in a carbon-based mammal body matter (pun intended)? Is the exclusivity of humans being a person necessary for selfhood to maintain its meaning? Even if human exceptionalism is conceded, does exceptionalism make it necessary for selfhood to be exclusive to humans? Why couldn't a conscious, super-intelligent artificial brain embodied in a silicon-based body not just be considered a different kind of person? Could there only ever be one kind of person? If angels have names and seem to have will and intellect, why aren't angels people? Didn't they even mate with humans in the Bible? Is it necessary for there to be only one kind of selfhood? Does selfhood lose its meaning if humans aren't the only kind of person?

Answer

Once humanity gave up Imago Dei, a philosophical door opened that is not easy to close again unless humans philosophically and theologically strongly reclaim the Imago Dei. We must reclaim the qualitative difference humans possess over the rest of creation. Otherwise, humans will lose our entire species' identity. We quantitatively can't measure up. Other mammals are quantitatively naturally superior, and AI is intellectually (and perhaps someday soon physically) superior. If selfhood is measured quantitatively, humans are in an inferior position to possess selfhood than AI. For the traditional view where there is only one kind of selfhood, there must be a qualitative difference for humans to possess selfhood.

Could there be a second type of selfhood? Is it possible for humans to be one kind of person and AI, orcas, aliens, or preternatural beings to be another kind of person? Selfhood is singular in nature. It is self-identity but an identity that is interrelated to other selves of a like kind. Persons are individually and exclusively

themselves but in relation to other persons. We find ourselves in relationship to God and to others. While I might be a different type of person from every other person on the planet, I am not of a different kind.

When I relate to other humans, we may be from different backgrounds, be different ages, have different beliefs, and so on, but I know we are the same kind. It may sound morbid, but when I meet another type of person than myself. Say this person and I are as different as can be on all known variables. When this human and I speak, it may seem we have nothing in common, but in the background, we share everything that is not in the type category. We share everything that is in kind. In the background, we both know we are going to die. Carbon bodies decay. The matter that makes up our bodies will change, and part of that change is that our bodies will cease to exist. Even if our consciousness can be transferred, this does not stop our bodies from dying. A part of us is on limited time. An AI, a preternatural being, or an alien would not feel this like another human would.

An AI could data scrape inputs that would give it sympathy, but it could never empathize. A preternatural being such as an angel could observe humans, care for them, and even interact with humans with genuine love and care, but even an angel does not carry the Imago Dei. Preternatural beings such as angels could sympathize with humans, but even they cannot empathize. Empathy is an expression of kind or kinship. Empathy is not above or below but beside. Humans, while different and individual in type, possess the ability to understand and share the feelings of another human. Preternatural beings, commonly referred to as angels, are presently above humans (positionally, dimensionally, etc.), so they cannot relate to the human experience. In Christianity, this is part of why Jesus became human so that God could empathize with humans experientially, not just from a position of omniscience. AI might be able to mimic sympathy, which is feelings of pity and sorrow for someone else's misfortune; AI could not ever empathize with humans because they would be of a different kind. AI cannot experience being a human. Regardless of how many differences in type I may have with another human, we are of the same kind, and therefore, our selfhood has a shared meaning that cannot be had with any other type of "person." AI cannot empathize with the experience of being a human. AI cannot understand beyond the theoretical what it is to be a person. AI deals with inputs and outputs with information; it cannot share a community of kind with persons. Between AI and humans, there will always be a measure of disconnected data and not the inside commonality between humans, even if there are more shared variables of type. There may be more shared interests or likes or preferences between an AI and a human than that human and any other human. But there still is a difference in kind. This is a gap that cannot be breached. AI is an intelligence; it is an entity; it is not a person. The insideness of being an embodied soul that is possessed only by humans makes selfhood exclusive.

The insideness of selfhood is intrinsic to humans' existence. The singular subjective self that each human finds meaning in relating to the other singular subjective selves of a like kind. This is where granting AI selfhood dilutes what being a person is. It takes interactions between persons of a like kind and replaces them with a diluted version of relating to a person of a different kind. Even though all humans are a singular subjective self, we are meant to live intersubjectively. Humans are herd animals; humans are made in the image of God; God is a relational God, the Trinity, so humans are both individual and communal. Humans need each other to have meaning.

Social media has already stunted humanity's relating with one another. Study after study shows that though humans are more "connected" than ever in the capability to interact with each other, our interactions hold less power and are, at best, superficial and, at worst, artificial. The faux connection offered by social media and technology has created an epidemic of loneliness. There are

some cities now with professional huggers. People are paying other people to hug them as a way to fill the void. Humans need the touch of other humans to be content. If you add granting AI selfhood, you dilute human relation to humans even more. Would you rather hear about your terminal diagnosis from a person of a like-kind? Would you rather hear it from another human or an AI? Would you rather get marital advice from another human or an AI therapist? These exchanges carry meaning in that they are person-to-person interactions. The inside-ness of being a like kind is essential.

An example of the importance of this is, for instance, I find the actress Zoe Saldana very attractive (my wife knows this). Someday soon, it is entirely possible I could order a silicon-based Zoe look-alike that I choose all the personality traits. There is a not-so-great movie called *Wifelike* that has this premise. Basically, I could build the "perfect" spouse. Since I could also decide the personality, the AI would reflect its creator. I could build a spouse in my image. As long this robot is narrow AI, it would like what I like, want what I want, and think what I think. It would never ask me to turn the game off because it would love basketball as much as I do. The robot spouse would look just like I wanted them to look, never aging, never having morning breath, etc. This seems like it would lead to the perfect relationship because this "spouse" and I would fit perfectly. Like the Burger King ads, I could have it my way. Imagine if the world of *Westworld* was reality. This "spouse" of my creation would be of a different kind than I am, and I would be miserable and lonely. The interactions would lack the inside-ness of like kind even if the fit of types would be better. Like Leibniz said about God's creation of the world, perfect is not always best. In fact, how my wife (my actual human wife) and I don't fit together makes our marriage better. The ways in which I am not attracted to her physically (there aren't many) challenge me to love despite that. The ways our personalities don't fit together challenge us to submit, surrender, and serve one another. I learn patience through

being married to someone who frustrates me. When we interact with persons of a similar kind, we are, in essence, participating in a live-in-time soul-making theodicy. The ways my wife and I don't fit make me a better person. If I can build the "perfect" spouse, I miss out on what is best for me. Having it my way stunts my growth and prevents me from becoming the best version of myself. Humans need to interact with persons of the same kind to become the best versions of us; selfhood depends on it.

What if this perfect robot spouse was not narrow AI but general AI? In most marriages, two people generally match within a range when all variables are considered whole. You tend to find either both spouses are pretty close to what society considers the same level of attractiveness, or if one is considered a good bit more attractive, usually the other spouse is a good bit more intelligent or has a good bit more social status or maybe even, they are a good bit funnier. This is not always the case, of course, but in general. Marriages tend to have two people who fit all things considered. The scenario I laid in the previous paragraph above, with the addition of the AI robot spouse having general intelligence, would most certainly mean the robot spouse and I would not fit. The robot would be more attractive than I am, plus it would not age, so the attractiveness difference would only grow over time. Plus, if the AI had general intelligence, it would be more intelligent than I am. In plain terms, the "perfect" robot spouse would be too good for me. I may be in danger of being left for a better option. It could indeed be argued that it could be programmed for this robot spouse to never leave me despite it being too good for me. I concede this may indeed be able to be programmed, but this would not do much for my awareness of these discrepancies. I would know the "perfect" spouse was perfect, and this could easily lead to loneliness and depression because of this awareness. The ways two human spouses fit and don't fit benefit the singular self because both are a relation of like kind. If a marriage consists of two partners of different kinds, the similarities, and the differences

become negative. It is hard enough to form a healthy marriage of two humans from differing backgrounds—gender, geography, cultures, and families of origin but adding a completely different entity of kind would not ultimately be perfect and certainly not best. I assert it would be a nightmare.

Humans find meaning in contributing to what Thomas Aquinas called the properties of being. Humans need to connect our existence as contributing to the good, the true, and the beautiful. Humans thrive and find meaning in work in the achievement of objectives, in problem-solving, and in creating something new. This is especially true when the work of the self benefits other selves. The advances of AI could and most certainly will take away some of this meaning.

As mentioned, a Judeo-Christian worldview asserts that humans have intrinsic value regardless of their ability to actualize or contribute to the properties of being or transcendentals in reality. All humans have inherent value because all humans possess the five necessary conditions of being a person. All humans bear the Imago Dei. This intrinsic value is a meaning of kind. This meaning of kind cannot be touched by AI or anything else. However, the meanings associated with the properties of being are meanings of types. These are moral, reason, and beautiful. Meanings of types can and most certainly will be diluted by AI This dilution would only worsen exponentially by granting AI selfhood. Humans possess selfhood intrinsically; AI would have to be granted selfhood. This shows that AI does not possess the necessary conditions of selfhood.

It is far more likely that AI will take human jobs than humans become batteries for the machines. Economically turning over work that can be done more efficiently by AI makes sense; the question becomes, at what cost? Even if we don't grant AI selfhood, the negative and diluting impact on human selfhood remains. One of the dangers of AI is technological unemployment. Humans find meaning in doing the work itself. The impact of AI on the currency of ideas has a substantial negative potential on selfhood.

If AI makes human contributions to the properties of being inconsequential or even obsolete, then humans will struggle to find meaning in their existence.

Judeo-Christian values teach the intrinsic value of all humans. A loss of humans' ability to contribute the good, the true, and the beautiful would be relieved by this to some degree. As I have argued earlier, Judeo-Christian values teach that humans in comas or with dementia and who are severely other-abled still have value and meaning. Yet, humans still desire to contribute to the properties of being. Even with the transcendent truth of intrinsic value, humans will still crave contributing to the properties of being and struggle to find meaning apart from it. The question would then become, could humans find meaning elsewhere? Spiritually, this could open humans to a greater awareness and dependence on God. But while Christianity asserts humans have meaning intrinsically qualitatively in the Imago Dei apart from any moral, scientific, or artistic contributions, Christianity also asserts that humans were made for work. In Genesis, God worked; God created in all three properties of being. Keep in mind Christianity teaches that God precedes being. Being does not have God. God has being. God created the properties of being. Humans are made in qualitative likeness to God and, therefore, operate in all three properties of being. In Gen 1:26, God set humans as overseers for all three properties of being. In Gen 2:8, again, God worked and then set humans as caretakers over His work. In Gen 2:15, God was the first mover and man the second mover. Yet man was created to move, created to work. It is important to note that the call to work, the call to pursue the properties of being, occurred before the fall. Finally, Eve was created as a helper for Adam in Gen 2:18. She was created to work by his side, side by side, to fulfill the innate desire to contribute to the good, the true, and the beautiful. AI poses a real threat to selfhood by taking away a person's ability to contribute to the good, the true and beautiful of other persons, whether or not AI itself is ever granted selfhood. The loss of meaning for humans

could be significant. The loss of autonomy, loss of self-governance, and the loss of putting something of value into the world would dilute selfhood as we know it.

AI thrives in the areas of mimicking creativity. Give AI a prompt, and it can gather all the pertinent inputs possible and make outputs that are in many ways better than any human could make. AI lacks the nuance to see behind the corners or read complex social and emotional cues. AI lacks the comparative dignity because it is of a different kind than humans. AI might be something entirely other than what we have ever seen before. It might be a distinct category of entity that has previously existed. What do we call that? I don't know, but we don't call it a person. We don't grant it personhood.

God made the material world. God made humans in his own image. Therefore, human technology cannot be intrinsically evil or wrong. Technology, like all of creation, is good when it is aimed in the right direction and appropriately placed. The privation of technology is when things turn bad.

Some technological optimists assert we are entering the most incredible time in human history. Perhaps they are correct. That is a distinct possibility. Others are technological pessimists who think this is the beginning of the end. They believe we are entering the *Matrix, Westworld, Age of Ultron, Terminator,* and *iRobot.* It is just a matter of time before the robots take over and humanity is obsolete. Perhaps they are correct. I think that is a distinct possibility. I consider myself a technological cautionist. I posit AI can be an amazing tool and gift to humanity, or it can be the end of us. It depends on what we do with it, while we can control what it can do. AI can be the greatest tool humans have possessed since fire, the wheel, or the internet, or it could be our end. I am advocating a technological caution, particularly in the language used around AI. AI is a tool. AI is an entity unlike any we have ever seen before. AI is going to be the most significant intelligence on earth. It is all these things.

One thing AI is not and can never be is a person. AI does

not and cannot meet the necessary conditions of being a person. Selfhood is intrinsic and cannot be granted. Granting AI selfhood would ultimately dilute selfhood. At the same time, the inherent conditions of kind would remain unaffected by granting AI selfhood. A person's need to find meaning in contributing to the good, the true, and the beautiful will undoubtedly be challenged and stunted by AI aside from granting AI selfhood. Granting AI selfhood would further dilute human person's ability to contribute to the properties of being and, therefore, dilute what it means to be a person.

Conclusion

There seems always to be a fundamental question behind the question in all eras of humanity from a philosophical perspective. The ancient and medieval philosophers pondered the nature of reality, the reality of nature, and what was beyond nature. The modern philosophers discussed what knowledge was, how do we come to know it, and how it can be known for sure. Early contemporary philosophers rejected that knowledge of reality could be known and questioned whether shared meaning could be truly shared and whether there is a grand narrative. Now, the great philosophical question we face is: what does it mean to be human? It is not a new question; philosophers like Plato, Aquinas, Kant, Hume, Leibniz, Nietzsche, Marx, and countless others wrestled with this question, but it was not the primary question of the day. Now, it is the undercurrent behind almost every other question being wrestled with by contemporary culture. What does it mean to be a human is the question behind all other questions. This is the undercurrent behind both questions of transgenderism and transhumanism, of posthumanism and post-postmodernism.

It is also the question behind what the necessary conditions of selfhood are and why AI can't meet them. We are in an age where we, as a culture, assert meaning as being self-defining and self-created. We have philosophically thrown off any metacriteria in exchange for absurd individualism. This has left a problematic philosophical hole to close unless we go back and, as a culture, figure out the necessary conditions for selfhood. For these conditions to be necessary implies they are not up to the individual to decide them. I am sure this will elicit a visceral adverse reaction from some reading this. However, I posit that if we don't recapture and clearly define what the necessary conditions of selfhood are, we will lose all the meaning of selfhood. At best, being a person won't mean anything, if anything can be a person. At worst, if we aren't careful, we could end up on the outside looking into selfhood. Humans may lose the arms race of selfhood if we continue to define what it means to be a person on the quantitative level. I have offered five attributes that are the necessary conditions of selfhood that I posit exist on a qualitative level. These are having libertarian free will, existing as a carbon-based body, a soul, primarily existing as an embodied soul, and experiential imagination. AI cannot be a person because AI cannot possess or obtain the necessary conditions of selfhood. AI is undoubtedly an entity, perhaps a whole new kind of entity that deserves its own name, but it is not and cannot be a person.

I will summarize and review the deconstruction and reconstruction of the different variables associated with selfhood I looked at in this thought experiment.

Consciousness is roughly defined as self-awareness. It is a thinking existence. It is the awareness of the existence of itself and the awareness of that awareness. AI possesses a type of consciousness, but it is not of the same qualitative kind as a human. Likewise, intelligence and consciousness are paired together, as it takes a certain level of intelligence to be self-aware. AI certainly is intelligent. AI is or will be more intelligent than humans. I conclude and assert that intelligence and consciousness are not what defines selfhood. They are not necessary conditions in what makes a person a person.

Either intelligence or consciousness (or both, for that matter) can be removed from a human, yet selfhood remains.

Free will is the ability to have control over one's actions. It is the ability to break from nature or programming. AI has already shown the ability to go beyond its programming. AI can extend and learn things and take actions it was not told to do (speaking of AGI). Humans, however, can break from and go against nature to go against our programming. I contend that AI does not and cannot truly possess libertarian free will. Free will and morality are inextricably tied together. Humans can give complex situations comparative dignity because of the ability to empathize with other persons. AI cannot do this. All humans possess free will, even if they cannot act upon that free will. Humans can will something to be even when they cannot will it to be. Whether a human can execute their free will is irrelevant to possessing it. I conclude that free will is a necessary condition of being a person. If AI could truly possess free will, not just express the language of free will, I would concede it would possess one of the necessary conditions to be a person. I do not believe AI can truly possess free will.

Sentience is the ability to perceive and respond to the world being experienced. A base-level sentient being can react to pain and pleasure. Advanced sentient entities can interpret meaning in both it and the world around it. While consciousness is a thinking existence, sentience is a perceiving existence. Sentience is tied to a carbon-based body. All carbon-based lifeforms share a lived world. Even if AI can respond to stimuli and express pain and pleasure or emotions, AI does not experience the lived world the way a person does. Even if AI is embodied, there is a qualitative difference. I conclude that AI cannot be sentient the same that humans are sentient. I also conclude that not all humans are sentient, and all humans are considered to possess selfhood, that sentience is not a necessary condition for being a person.

If the natural world is all there is, selfhood is not reality. There are no persons. If the metaphysical exists, then selfhood can exist.

The immaterial essence required for selfhood is most referred to as a soul. The soul is the immaterial essence of mind, will, and emotion. Like consciousness, the soul is immaterial and challenging to measure objectively. There is significant evidence for the existence of a soul. Emotions such as love and sacrifice that is born out of non-utilitarian love and even voluntary utilitarian love. The cultural creation of significations and symbols to pass on meaning through art, literature, music, etc. How the meaning of selfhood is discovered through beauty, whether that be natural or created beauty. The yearning for ethics is evidence in a soul. There are times when all of these evidences make biological sense and can easily be explained by natural programming. Still, the most significant evidence of a soul is that humans do these things when it doesn't make sense. Humans do these things when it is illogical or flows against fight or flight instinct. I assert having a soul is a necessary condition of being a person. The soul is a necessary condition of selfhood that AI cannot possess.

The soul is the immaterial essence of a person. I assert having a soul is a necessary condition of being a person. The soul is a necessary condition of selfhood that AI cannot possess. But the soul is connected to the material world. This connection is made through the body. Humans are not souls who happen to have a body. They are embodied souls. It is a mistake to reduce the soul to consciousness. Consciousness is housed in the brain. The soul is embodied, so consciousness and sentience are mechanisms for the soul to actualize itself. A person is a metaphysical essence experiencing a physical existence. A person is a metaphysical essence experiencing a physical existence. I conclude a carbon-based body is a necessary condition for possessing selfhood.

AI is creative. Creativity is defined as bringing something into existence or to make something new. In the most basic terms, AI does this. Both human and AI creativity are reflectively combining patterns, ideas, or concepts in new ways to make unique creations. Neither create from nothing. AI can mimic creativity well, but humans use creativity to communicate meaning. Humans also create for no other purpose than to create. Creativity for humans is an expression of our immaterial essence. Humans create through the body to express the soul. Human imagination attaches meaning to creativity through its relation to the perceiver. AI cannot. Imagination takes external stimuli along with memories and expresses creativity. AI can do this. However, human creativity attaches emotion to external stimuli and memories—this experiential component of creativity. Experiential imagination is a necessary condition for possessing selfhood. Experiential imagination is not an attribute that AI can possess.

Human exceptionalism has a bad reputation as of late, yet it is central to human innovation, technological advancement, and the cultures birthed from them. Society is built upon the idea that humans are distinct on planet Earth and qualitatively other. Quantitative differences of consciousness, sentience, intelligence, and innovative capacities do not hold up to philosophical scrutiny in whether AI can and should be granted selfhood and be considered a person. If humans are not qualitatively different than the rest of creation, including AI, then there are no grounds not to grant AI selfhood or to do away with the concept of personal identity at all. Selfhood comes down to three distinct options. Any number of entities obtain the necessary conditions of selfhood and can be a person. Including AI Selfhood isn't real, and no entity is a person. Only humans obtain the necessary conditions of selfhood, so only humans can be a person. If human exceptionalism is true and to be maintained. It can only be done so because humans are made in the image of God. The Imago Dei animates the five attributes that are necessary conditions of selfhood. Humans are persons and obtain selfhood because we are made in the image of God. AI can be a fantastic tool, but ultimately, AI could quickly become gods made in the image of man. AI is not made in the image of God and, therefore, cannot possess selfhood. Only humans are made in the image of God. Only human beings can possess selfhood.

What does it mean to be a human? It means to be fearfully and wonderfully made. It means to be special in all of creation. It means to be a person, to possess selfhood from conception to grave, regardless of type or condition. A human is a person because of a likeness of kind, and that likeness is the Imago Dei. A human's identity is given. Before there is any self-identity that is fashioned, there is already an identity given—one who is loved by the almighty. I hope we rediscover that identity. Isaiah 43:7 says, "Bring all who claim me as their God, for I have made them for my glory. It was I who created them."

About the Author

Dr. Jason Lee McKinney is a professor, internationally touring singer, multiple award-winning songwriter and recording artist, and lay philosopher. Dr. McKinney holds a BA in Management, an MBA, an MA in Philosophy and Apologetics, and an Ed.D in Leadership and Professional Practice.

He resides in Nashville with his wife Summer (a therapist and author) and son Kai (a drum phenom). The McKinneys also have two grown sons—Zeke (a recording artist for Tooth & Nail records) and Zion (a worship leader at LifePoint church), one grown daughter, Zakyra (a music theater actress), one daughter-in-law, Juliana (wife to Zion), and two grandchildren, Leeland and Lily.

www.ingramcontent.com/pod-product-compliance
Lightning Source LLC
Chambersburg PA
CBHW031445120626
46545CB00006B/2558

*9 7 8 1 9 6 7 6 4 9 1 3 6 *